THE COMPLETE

GILBERT AND SULLIVAN

THE COMPLETE
GILBERT AND SULLIVAN

CHARLES BUCHEL

DIANA BELL

THE WELLFLEET PRESS
WELLFLEET

A QUARTO BOOK

Published by Wellfleet Press
110 Enterprise Avenue
Secaucus, New Jersey 07094

ISBN 1-55521-440-1

This book was designed and produced by
Quarto Publishing plc
The Old Brewery
6 Blundell Street
London N7 9BH

Art Director: Ian Hunt
Editorial Director: Jeremy Harwood
Photography: Alex Saunderson
Indexer: Hazel Bell

Typeset by
Central Southern Typesetters, Eastbourne
Manufactured in Hong Kong by
Regent Publishing Services Limited
Printed in Hong Kong by
South Sea International Press Ltd

Quarto would like to thank the D'Oyly Carte
Opera Trust and the New D'Oyly Carte Opera
Company for their invaluable and sympathetic
assistance in the preparation of this book. The
majority of the photographs come from the
D'Oyly Carte Trust, others were provided by Mrs
Mary Godfrey, widow of the late Isadore Godfrey.

I would like to thank the staff at the D'Oyly Carte
offices for their patience with my disruptive
presence in their midst, and in particular
Margaret Bowden for her helpful and
encyclopaedic answers to my questions. My
thanks to Mrs Mary Godfrey for her loan of
invaluable material and her vivid reminiscences
of her husband's long career with the company.
My abiding gratitude to my long-suffering
husband, Peter Swann, for his painstaking and
percipient proof-reading and criticism of the
text. DB

Contents

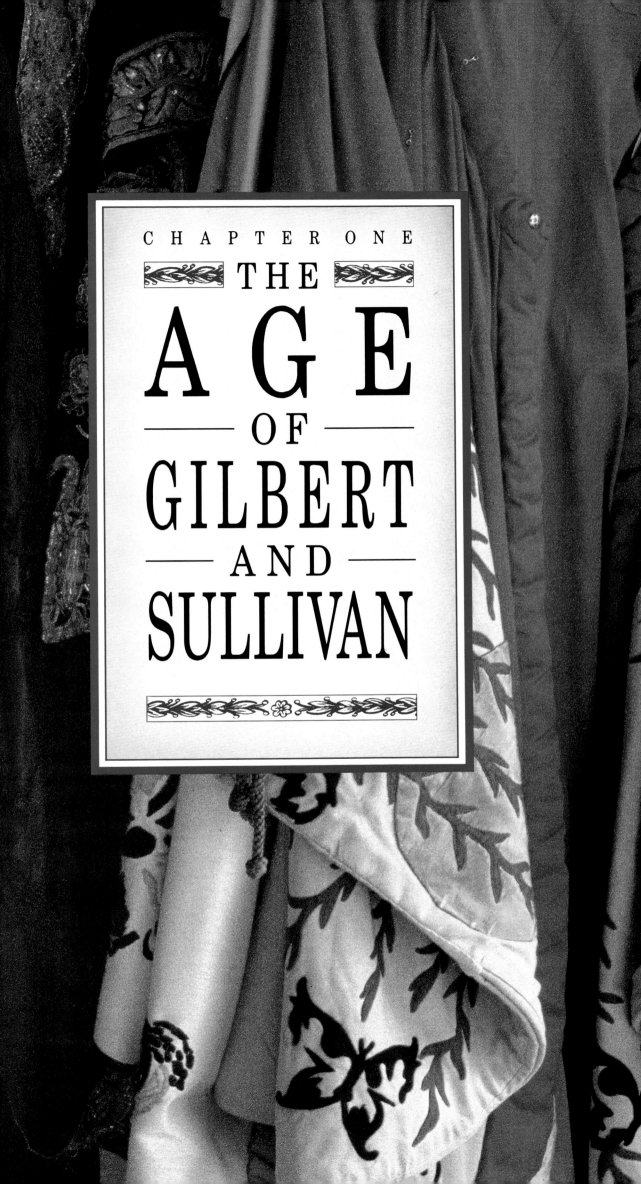

CHAPTER ONE

THE AGE OF GILBERT AND SULLIVAN

"When I was a lad, I served a term as office boy to an attorney's firm". Gilbert's vision of Sir Joseph Porter KCB, First Lord of the Admiralty, at his clerk's desk at the start of his career, as related in HMS Pinafore. The character of Sir Joseph is based on that of W.H. Smith, the First Lord in Disraeli's Conservative administration (above).

"When the night wind howls". A vivid illustration of the pleasures of the "ghosts' high noon", the theme of Sir Roderic's celebrated song in Act II of Ruddigore (below)

THE VICTORIAN POLITICIAN Disraeli's pronouncement that the British were divided into two nations – the rich and the poor – had been true throughout the 18th century and was a fact of life that was certainly reflected in the nature of theatrical audiences during the earlier part of Victoria's reign. Over the next 50 years, however, a prosperity boom changed the nature of society, with a vast increase in the number of respectable citizens – ranging from small tradesmen to rich industrialists. These made up the High Victorian middle class.

As far as the theatre was concerned, the effects were dramatic. Improved education meant better audience understanding, while increased prosperity meant more spending, especially on entertainment. The result was a kaleidoscopic shift in the pattern of the Victorian audience.

THE THEATRE AND ITS AUDIENCE

The uniquely memorable Gilbert and Sullivan operas were to emerge from this time of reform and review. They were not, as it sometimes appears, an apparently isolated phenomenon in a desert of musical mediocrity and theatrical vulgarity, but were rather the end product of the reformatory work of writers and managers whose names are mostly forgotten today.

In the first part of the 19th century, the only theatrical fare suitable for what was loosely termed "polite" society was to be found at the so-called "patent" theatres – Drury Lane and Covent Garden. They were termed "patent" because they were still the only theatres licensed by an Act of Parliament passed in 1737 to perform Shakespeare or the standard dramatic repertoire. Grand opera was limited to Her Majesty's Theatre. Literary merit had deserted the drama. It was to be found in the works of the Romantic poets, who did not write plays that were theatrically viable, or in the novel. Entertainment therefore tended to be domestic-based, with voracious reading of fine fiction as the norm in the middle-class family circle – this, after all, was the age of Dickens, the Brontës and Thackeray. Magazine reading, too, was on the increase, leading examples being the surprisingly radical magazine, *Fun*, to which Gilbert frequently contributed, together with its milder contemporary, *Punch*. Grand opera as a performance was popular only with the upper classes, but home music-making, as indicated by the soaring sales of cheap upright pianos, was universal. The family was all-important: it was kept unsullied from the steamy entertainment world outside the "patent" theatres.

Sexually Puritan in theory, the potential audience of the day was less so in practice. It is typical that high society quietly accepted Sullivan's lifelong liaison with Mrs Ronalds because she was separated from her husband, and Sullivan was a bachelor. The open honesty of divorce was regarded as a social stigma. Even in 1878,

Captain Corcoran's "Damn" in *HMS Pinafore* aroused considerable offence; equally the original title of *Ruddigore* – *Ruddygore* – ruffled Victorian susceptibilities.

The general theatrical audience, as opposed to that of the "patent" theatres, was three-tier: firstly, the rich men about town, usually on the prowl for young actresses who were often regarded as unofficial prostitutes (even the eminently respectable Jenny Lind was denied entry to John Ruskin's house before she became famous); secondly, the shadier end of artistic society: thirdly the audience's heart, the so-called working class, who had fought in the theatre riots at the beginning of the century for space in the pit and against rising ticket prices.

Obviously the type of entertainment was dictated by the wishes of this audience, and the exigences of the licensing laws. Gilbert knew this when he said in an interview in 1885 for the *Daily News:* "except in the case of Shakespeare or of French adaptation, English dramatists are driven within the narrow limits of bourgeois thought imposed by the survival of Puritanical prejudice. The English dramatist dances his hornpipe in fetters".

APPEALING TO THE AUDIENCE

The most popular theatrical forms were burletta, burlesque, melo-drama and pantomime, sharing many characteristics, in particular, so-called spectacles – Gilbert knew all about this when he specified incongruous "Red Fire" at the end of *Trial by Jury* – and the use of popular songs taken from music-hall vaudevilles, or lifted from the opéra-bouffes of composers such as Offenbach.

The typical burletta, for instance, contained five or six well-known tunes in each act, with new words, which were often racy or satirical. They were part of the natural action and not forced into it. The burletta's pedigree can be traced back to the venerable tradition of English ballad opera, especially John Gay's *Beggar's Opera* of the previous century, where the satire was more pointed, and the subject more openly licentious than in any 19th-century work, but where contemporary popular tunes of the time also featured heavily.

The burlesque, often called an extravaganza, was based on mock classical subjects, which were intended to appeal to the more edu-cated part of the audience, with titles like *Midas* (by K. O'Hara), or Charles Dibden's *Poor Vulcan*. The joke lay in a revered figure behaving in an all-too-human manner. Gilbert couched *Thespis* in this form, with his bronchitic and galoshes-shod Gods. The same idea was constantly used in opéra-bouffe. Other revered figures were equally pilloried; Shakespeare was frequently burlesqued, as were Bellini and Donizetti, the current idols of Italian grand opera. Bellini's *La Sonnambula* became *The Supper, the Sleeper and the Merry Swiss Boy*, while the unfortunate *Lucia di Lammer-moor* was expanded into *The Lady, the Laird and the Lover* by

The Waterloo Gallery, Windsor Castle, stands ready for a Royal Command Gilbert and Sullivan performance. Queen Victoria loved the theatre and was an ardent Savoyard.

"*She may very well pass for 43 in the dusk with the light behind her*" *Gilbert's "rich attorney" introduces his "elderly, ugly daughter" to the Judge in the early days of his career (Trial by Jury) (below).*

that merciless alliterator, H. J. Byron. Gilbert, while still a dramatic apprentice in his craft, burlesqued Meyerbeer's *Robert le Diable* for John Hollingshead, who was later to put on *Thespis* at the Gaiety theatre, which frequently staged Offenbach burlesques. Nor was the Victorian age's favourite poet immune from Gilbert's shafts of ridicule. In his "per-version" of Tennyson's *The Princess*, he added insult to injury by introducing Figaro's *Largo el Factotum* from Rossini's *The Barber of Seville*, with his own words. His best known extravaganza, however, was on *L'Elisir d'Amore*, with the splendidly Gilbertian sub-title of *Dulcamara*, or *the Little Duck or the Great Quack*.

MELODRAMA AND PANTOMIME

Melodrama, later to be the inspiration of *Ruddigore*, had always been popular, especially when crime and social injustice were the subjects, as in the classics *Maria Marten*, produced around 1830, and *Sweeney Todd*, produced in 1847. As late as 1868, *London by Gaslight* thrilled the audience at the Adelphi.

Pantomime, with its traditional elements, maintained its perennial hold, but at this stage was certainly no family entertainment. James Robinson Planché (1796–1880) was its main exponent, though Gilbert himself wrote one for the 1867–8 season entitled *Harlequin Cock and Jenny Wren*. He crafted this lowly plot carefully, but, even so, it was interrupted for "The Fairy Aquarium" (with ballet), the "Spectacles of St James Park After a Snowstorm" followed by an "Electric Light and Magic Fountain patented by M. Delaporte of Paris!" Gilbert's revenge was to lampoon pantomime and its intermezzi of irrelevancy in the next issue of *Fun*. The pantomime elements of demon king, magic potions, principal boy, preferably with good legs, and pantomime dame were still to be found in the Savoy Operas' stereotype characters. John Wellington Wells (*The Sorcerer*) could have been a demon king, while Nanki-Poo was later played as a principal boy in America. Gilbert's numerous unloveable middle-aged ladies – Katisha, Ruth, Lady Jane and so on – are only up-market pantomime dames.

THEATRICAL REFORMS

In 1843 the Theatre Regulation Act was passed, ending the monopoly of the "patent" theatres. This liberating measure meant that minor theatres no longer were forced to limit themselves to song and dance entertainment and ushered in a great surge of theatrical reform. Squire Bancroft, with his wife Marie, introduced generally acceptable plays of a drawing-room comedy genre at the Prince of Wales. He also acted in the plays of Tom Robertson (1829–71) who, from 1865, desperately tried to introduce some realism into the theatre and improve dramatic standards.

"I *am the very model of a modern Major-General". The character of Gilbert's Victorian polymath in The Pirates of Penzance was based on that of Sir Garnet Wolesley, the military hero of the day (above).*

"M*y name is John Wellington Wells, I'm a dealer in magic and spells". The Sorcerer's central character introduces himself in the partnership's first great patter song, cataloguing his wares (above).*

G*ilbert and Sullivan mania swept Victorian England and the United States. This cigarette card collection illustrates characters from the major Savoy operas. The operas featured are Iolanthe, The Mikado, The Pirates of Penzance, The Gondoliers, Princess Ida and Patience (right).*

"O *foolish fay, think you because". Captain Shaw quenches the fires of the Fairy Queen's love for a mortal in Iolanthe. The real Captain Shaw, head of the London Fire Brigade, attended the glittering Savoy first night (above).*

"I*f you give me your attention". Princess Ida's father, King Gama, made a profession out of being disagreeable (below).*

Robertson's plays were dubbed "teacup and saucer", just as in this century John Osborne was designated a "kitchen sink" drama-tist. He believed in ensemble playing, not just a star system, and his simple titles – *Society, Ours* and, above all, *Caste* have an attack which must have jolted the Victorian audiences into facing social reality. He and Gilbert were friends: Gilbert paid public tribute to him as "an exceedingly skilful dramatic tailor ... he fitted each character with the utmost nicety to the man or woman who was to play in it; and he was there to instruct them in every movement, every emphasis ... he invented stage-management ... showed how to give life and variety and nature to the scene by breaking it up with all sorts of little incidents and delicate by-play. I have been at many of his rehearsals and learnt a great deal from them". Robert-son's ideals were to influence Gilbert all his life.

Another "realistic" playwright was Dion Boucicault (1822–90), who had an excellent theatrical sense and cultivated naturalism in his Irish comedies. His plays were often used as a basis for libretti, and Gilbert mentions him in the Colonel's song in *Patience* – "The pathos of Paddy as rendered by Boucicault". Some elements from the plot of one of his plays, *Don César de Bezan*, were later incor-porated into *The Yeomen of the Guard*.

"ASSUMPTIONS" AND "ILLUSTRATIONS"

The hypocrisy of his audience was well-understood by the impre-sario and actor German Reed, who carefully avoided the word "play" by substituting "illustration", and called his roles "assumptions", thus introducing a positively sanctimonious air to the stage. His respectable audiences, or "gatherings", made the entertainments at his "Gallery of Illustration" sound like Sunday school lectures. They were so respectable that they were frequented by clergymen and spinsters, who enjoyed piano recitalists, non-risqué cabaret acts, domestic scenes and one-act operettas. His Gallery was the scene of Gilbert and Sullivan's first meeting at a rehearsal of *Ages Ago*, Frederic Clay's opera to Gilbert's libretto: Gilbert was to recycle the plot for *Ruddigore*. Sullivan was one of Reed's composers: he wrote the music for Burnand's *La Contrabandista* and, more memorably, *Cox and Box*, which shared the bill with Gilbert's *No Cards* on 29 March 1869.

These educated and polite audiences had different require-ments in the theatre. Irving darkened the auditorium at the Lyceum, Gilbert popularised matinées at the Savoy, and detailed programmes, not playbills, were provided at Wyndhams. The hours of perform-ance, which had been 6.30pm to 11pm, were altered to accommodate a dining clientele, while the evening bill was substantially curtailed, though the habit of a curtain-raiser was to persist throughout the hey-day of the Savoy operas. Seats were reserved or queued for in the pit and gallery, which were the working-class preserves, though gradually the pit, after much protest, became the orchestra stalls. The dress circle and upper circle were also established, though the gallery was retained. The dress in more expensive seats was white tie for the men and diamonds for the women. Above all Queen Victoria herself was a frequent attender in the 1850s before Albert's death, and the royal seal of approval meant a new clean theatrical bill of health.

But the audience was still affected by the class-system, and this awareness was to colour the subject matter of many of the libretti and plays of the time. William Bagehot in *The English Constitution* wrote in 1850 that "every class of society accepts with cheerfulness the lot which Providence has assigned to it; while at the same time, each individual of each class is constantly trying to raise himself in the social scale". Lord Palmerston in an 1865 speech said that, in every sphere, "men have risen to the highest points who have themselves started from the smallest beginning", while Robertson was succinct in *Caste:* "Caste is a good thing if it's not carried too far. It shuts the door on the pretentious and the vulgar: but it should open wide for exceptional merit." Audiences sympathized with such sentiments, which Gilbert was to echo.

A Plethora of Theatres

Because of the variety of material that was being produced, the theatre buildings of the time had different appearances and traditions. This was the age of the actor-manager – Irving was at the Lyceum, and, later, Beerbohm Tree at Her Majesty's. On a lower level, John Hollingshead opened at the Gaiety in 1868, and made it the home of English burlesque (he was later to condemn Gilbert and Sullivan opera as "burlesque in long clothes"). He had a troupe of repertory actors, who specialised in different roles: Nellie Farren was one of these, and undoubtedly the first night audience at *Thespis* had come to gape at her legs as she played Mercury, unaware that they were assisting at the birth of one of light opera's most historic occasions, the first partnership of Gilbert and Sullivan.

By 1885, Hollingshead had managed to clean up the shows, and was joined by George Edwardes. Together they were to establish musical comedy as an accepted dramatic form. Hollingshead used electric light before its historic use at the Savoy, though only on the roof of the theatre as a primitive battery-run searchlight to illuminate the surrounding streets. Unfortunately the streets were soon plunged into darkness again, as there were complaints that the carriage-horses were frightened. Programmes were perfumed, there was a good restaurant, and tipping of the staff was no longer compulsory. It was a transformation as spectacular as any on the London stage.

Other theatres feature frequently in the play bills of the time. The Lyceum always had very fashionable audiences, but the fore-

THE FLOWERS THAT BLOOM IN THE SPRING, TRA LA,
BREATHE PROMISE OF MERRY SUNSHINE,
AS WE MERRILY DANCE AND WE SING, TRA LA,
WE WELCOME THE HOPE THAT THEY BRING, TRA LA,
OF A SUMMER OF ROSES AND WINE.
AND SO, COATS' SPOOL COTTON IS ALWAYS A THING
AS WELCOME AS FLOWERS THAT BLOOM IN THE SPRING.

"The flowers that bloom in the Spring". Or in this case, the virtues of Coats cotton, which Nanki-Poo is advertising.

"I have a song to sing O!" Jack Point, the "merryman" of The Yeomen of the Guard, looses the love of his "merrymaid" to Colonel Fairfax (below).

most straight comedy theatre was the Haymarket, managed by the Bancrofts who succeeded, at the cost of a first night riot, to jettison the pit. The Prince of Wales opened in 1884 featuring serious modern dramatists, such as Ibsen, but later produced burlesques and the first musical comedy, *In Town*. The Old Vic, in Waterloo Road, had a very lurid reputation until taken over by a philanthropist, Miss Emma Cons, who converted it into a cheap, cheerful, teetotal and essentially polite venue.

Gilbert and Sullivan first nights were *Thespis* at the Gaiety, *Trial by Jury* at the Royalty in Soho, *The Sorcerer* at the Opera Comique, followed by *HMS Pinafore*, *The Pirates of Penzance* and *Patience*. The last was to transfer to the partnership's new permanent home – the Savoy. The Royalty was historically important for its unsuccessful trial of the first moving stage in 1840, whose internal machinery, aided by the efforts of a sturdy horse, caused the whole building to vibrate so violently that it had to be rebuilt! In 1850 it was the scene of a brief effort to establish a permanent home for a native school of English grand opera by the composer Balfe, and in the 1860s, a school of acting. *Trial by Jury's* first performance there in 1875 was not part of any significant theatrical policy.

The Opéra-Comique had opened in 1871 with D'Oyly Carte's own musical play after Molière's *Le Médecin Malgré Lui*, which failed. Little else of note appeared until Carte put on *The Sorcerer*, and after its brief hour of operatic glory with the premières of the other operas in the Gilbert and Sullivan pantheon up to *Patience*, it closed. It was an incredibly uncomfortable theatre – rickety and out-of-date. Tunnels from four different streets led to its entrance and these were either draughty or too hot, and at risk from fire.

This last was a common problem. Many badly-built theatres were gutted by fire, as a result of the use of naked gas lighting, so D'Oyly Carte's introduction of electric light at the Savoy was a milestone in theatrical safety. He completed the theatre in October 1881. Electricity, however, was not used until 28 December, when Carte appeared dramatically on the stage with an electric light bulb shrouded in muslin, and after giving a lecture on its safety, smashed it to prove that the muslin did not burn; only one member of the audience rushed out of the theatre in terror.

The Savoy was bigger than the Opera-Comique, seating 1,300, and was one of the first theatres to be constructed on the cantilever principle, giving an excellent view of the stage from every seat. There were numerous entrances and exits for safety, while the tickets had both a seating plan and seat location printed on their stubs. Orderly queues at the box-office were instituted, and programmes and cloakrooms were free. The decor was "neither Queen Anne nor early English, free equally from gingerbread or cherubim" said Carte, who had simply, but tastefully, decorated it in white, pale yellow and gold with a quilted silk curtain. The whole achieve-

D'*Oyly Carte playbills from the 1920s. The opera company Carte founded was to become a British institution (left).*

T*he Savoy's palatial 1880s interior. It was the first London theatre to be lit by electricity (top).*

T*he Savoy before and during its 1920s rebuilding (centre and above).*

The partnerships' business accounts make fascinating reading. Gilbert and Sullivan was profitable for decades until the copyrights expired.

ment certainly merited the appearance of the Prince of Wales in the Royal Box, though there is some query over the date of his first visit – it may have been on 9 December, rather than on the opening night. It was from this theatre that Carte was to build his empire, and make the fortunes of the Savoy partnership.

THE "LAND WITHOUT MUSIC"

Victorian England suffered from a musical inferiority complex. It was contemptuously dismissed by the Germans as "the land without music", for, ever since the advent of Handel in 1710, the native musical tradition had lost its creative confidence as far as serious composition was concerned. There were still performances in plenty and the audiences were musically aware, but any home-grown talent was automatically regarded as second rate. The German tradition dominated in sacred music, the symphony and concerto; here Mendelssohn, England's adopted son, reigned with bland and creamy professionalism, even over such essentially English institutions as the Leeds or the Three Choirs Festivals. The roll-call of indigenous talent amongst Sullivan's contemporaries contains many semi-forgotten names: Stainer (1840–1901), the composer of *The*

Crucifixion, A.C. Mackenzie (1847–1935), Sterndale Bennett (1816–1875), and J. C. Curwen (1847–1916), whose father invented the tonic sol-fa system, are among their number. They were to be followed by the infinitely more impressive figures of Parry (1848–1918), Stanford (1852–1924) and eventually Elgar (1857–1934). Sullivan himself was regarded as the first English composer worthy of following in Mendelssohn's footsteps, in that his easy seriousness, his immediate sentiment (not necessarily synonymous with sentimentality), and his comfortably stirring, but never disturbing, music summed up all that was enjoyed by the contemporary audience. Music was basically occasional – in other words, a necessary part of the panoply of state or civic occasions – and Sullivan's output fitted the bill admirably. So, when he began to dabble with light opera with *Cox and Box,* the move was brushed aside by the critics as an amusing bonne-bouche amongst his normal musical fare.

CONTEMPORARY OPERA

As far as serious opera was concerned, the new romantic school of Weber, Lortzing and Marschner, which was to flower into the overwhelming musical personality of Wagner in the second part of the 19th century, was accepted, while the inflated melodramas of Meyerbeer and the sentimentality of Gounod were much admired. But the vocal brilliance of Italian grand opera reigned supreme. Verdi became popular from the 1850s – and there are many Verdian echoes in Sullivan's more serious moments.

However, there was a modest English opera school led by Michael Balfe (1803–1870), Julius Benedict (1804–1885), and Vincent Wallace (1814–1865), who, between them, produced a trio of

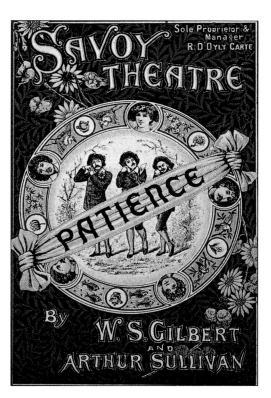

T*he new main entrance of the rebuilt Savoy, photographed at night. Here, 1920s elegance met Victorian tradition to mutual benefit.*

T*he elaborate front-of-house playbill for Patience. Rupert D'Oyly Carte followed the reforming footsteps of his father in his determination to keep the theatre up-to-date (above).*

D'OYLY CARTE

THE GONDOLIERS

THE MIKADO

THE YEOMEN OF THE GUARD

OPERA COMPANY

This hoarding-sized poster is still preserved in the present company's warehouse. Rupert's gift for advertising, as demonstrated in these striking designs, did much to keep the operas popular (above).

operas known as the "English Ring". Balfe's *Bohemian Girl* (1843) had all the elements that audiences enjoyed at that time, with a romantic plot remote from everyday life and larger-than-life prot-agonists. Boucicault's play *The Lily of Killarney* was the basis of Benedict's opera of the same name (1862), while the same drama-tist's *Don César de Bezan*, lay behind the libretto of Wallace's *Maritana* (1845). Sullivan was later to be accused of copying this work in *The Yeomen of the Guard*. Though it contains some comic elements, it again deals with either the very rich or the very poor. All three of these operas were immediately performed in America with great success – a pattern that was to be repeated in the Savoy operas from *HMS Pinafore* onwards.

THE INFLUENCE OF OFFENBACH

None of these composers wrote true light opera. This field was dominated by a Franco-German, Jacques Offenbach (1819–1880), who defined his works as opéra-bouffe, though he also called his frothy entertainments vaudeville, revue and even "opéra-féerique" or "fairy opera", a genre that was to influence *Iolanthe*.

Offenbach felt that the leading contemporary opéra-comique composers – Adam, Thomas and Auber – had lost their way amongst the confusing nomenclature of opera buffa and opéra-comique and created a hybrid of comic and grand opera. He wanted to return to a "genre primitif et gai". In his works, he aimed to give his public good melodies and original ideas, yet retained the ability to be brief and simple. To this end, he constantly satirised classical antiquity, as in his best known works, *Orpheus in the Underworld* (produced in London as *Orpheus in the Underground* in 1865) and *La Belle Hélène* (produced in London as *Or Taken from the Greek* in 1866). Another characteristic was pungent political satire, as in *La Grande Duchesse de Gérolstein*, produced in London in 1867 and referred to in Gilbert and Sullivan's *The Grand Duke*. He even satirises sexual excess in the 1866 *Bluebeard*. It is notable that Wagner, whose manifold gifts did not include an ability to mock either himself or others, said, "his music has the warmth of the dung-pile in which all the swine of Europe could wallow."

Offenbach did not live to see the 1881 first performance of his one serious masterpiece, *The Tales of Hoffmann*. He was the arch-enemy of Romanticism and self-importance. The German philosopher Nietzsche, of all people, loved his logical but high-spirited buffoonery and said he had a "divine ease" and "inimitable effervescence". That acid perfectionist, George Bernard Shaw, was in agreement and admired his "restless movement, witty abandonment, swift light wicked touch, the inimitable sly élan stealing into concerted pieces as light as puff paste".

THE SAVOY SCHOOL

The term opéra-bouffe became synonymous with operetta which Saint-Saëns described as "a daughter of opéra-comique, a daughter who has turned out badly, but daughters who have turned out badly are not without charm". Gilbert himself said that, when he started to collaborate with Sullivan, "English comic opera had practically ceased to exist, and such musical entertainments that held the stage were adaptations of operas by Offenbach, Auber, Lecocq, Planquette and Hervé. Their treatment was crude, unintelligent and sometimes frankly improper."

Gilbert and Sullivan were to take what they needed from all these types of opera. From opéra-comique and opéra-bouffe, they took spoken dialogue (except in *Trial by Jury*), patter-songs, semi-military songs of heroic young men and fast waltz-time finales. Sullivan admired grand opera enough to parody it wickedly and successfully. Gilbert took political and social satire from Offenbach and softened it, while removing the open sexual innuendo which would have scandalised his newly-respectable audience, who were now informed enough to appreciate wit without wickedness, and humour without heartlessness.

"A *magnet hung in a hardware shop". Grosvenor's fable of the magnet and the churn in Patience baffles his attentive audience of love-sick maidens, but reflects his love for the opera's heroine (above).*

"W*e are peers of highest station". Top hats from Iolanthe and other items of headgear piled into a skip ready for storage.*

CHAPTER TWO

THE BIRTH OF A TRADITION

I
N THE PREVIOUS CENTURY, 17 Southampton Street, Strand had belonged to a gentleman who had, according to his grandson "known Dr Johnson, Garrick and Reynolds and who was the last man in London ... who wore Hessian boots and a pigtail". He was even reputed to be descended from the Elizabethan adventurer Sir Humphrey Gilbert. This grandson was born on 18 November 1836 and was christened William Schwenk Gilbert. His unresponsively cold mother, a Scottish doctor's daughter, and his argumentative Royal Navy surgeon father were always quarrelling, and eventually parted when Gilbert was 19 – he always sympathised with his father, who had taken up a second career as an author on retirement. Perhaps the latter's profuse, moralistic and stilted literary outpourings were a bone of contention in the marriage. The lack of distinction in the father's literary career was to be balanced by his son's spectacular success.

CHILDHOOD, SCHOOL AND THE BAR

Not a great deal is known of Gilbert's childhood, apart from one bizarre event which clearly left its imprint on his mind. The family were on holiday in Italy, and the nanny of the two-year-old "Bab", as the young Gilbert was nicknamed, was persuaded by a couple of plausible ruffians to hand over the toddler, who was immediately ransomed by his father for £25 – an incident whose haphazard unreality was to figure in both *The Pirates of Penzance* and *The Gondoliers*.

Gilbert's schooldays were spent at the Great Ealing School, where he took part in school dramatics as both author and actor, but was apparently lazy until his naturally competitive spirit asserted itself, and he became a reasonably academic head boy. The extent of his interest in the stage is illustrated by his attempt at 15 to persuade Charles Kean, the most famous actor-manager of the day, to employ him, but Kean naturally enough refused. While an undergraduate at King's College, London, Gilbert limited his dramatic aspirations to the unlikely conversion of the erstwhile Scientific Society into a Dramatic Society of which he was the secretary!

In 1854 the Crimean War broke out, and Gilbert studied for the competitive examination for a commission into the Royal Artillery. Though the army and navy in general were always one of his satiric targets, he was still fascinated both by service life and by the lure of uniform. Later, he joined the 5th West Yorkshire Militia and then became a captain in the Royal Aberdeenshires – both were volunteer forces raised to supplement Britain's tiny regular army in time of national emergency. But, for Gilbert, the call never came and the end of the Crimean War in 1856 left him drifting and motiveless.

Having gained his degree in that year, Gilbert frittered away four unproductive years as an Assistant Clerk in the Privy Council Office's Education Department, which he was to pronounce "ill

Arthur Sullivan, photographed in middle age. "The bright, genial composer" of the Savoy operas was the darling of Victorian society; however, his serious music, such as his oratorio "The Light of the World" and his grand opera "Ivanhoe" has not survived its times; the last professional revival of "Ivanhoe" was by Sir Thomas Beecham's opera company in the early 1900s.

A*rthur Sullivan,*
complete with his
inseparable monocle. He
was the bright young hope
of serious British music,
but his work with Gilbert
was frowned on by many
of his peers.

organised and ill-governed" in an article in *Theatre* many years later. He said that his salary of £120 a year was "one of the worst bargains any government ever made!" A legacy of £300 seemed to provide him with an escape, and he turned to the law as a career. The following disastrous six years of grubbing a living as an unsuccessful barrister ending up on the Northern Circuit were later to yield unimagined financial reward as the source of so many ideas in the Savoy operas. He even used one incident in a short story for the *Cornhill* magazine; when he had miserably lost one of the average of five cases he had a year, and his furiously disappointed client threw her boot at him in court after her sentence.

Gilbert's failure to impress the court was perhaps because he was naturally a nervous and indecisive speaker; he became more skilful later in life. His average legal earnings in the early 1860s were £75 per annum – a far cry from the £40,000 a year he was to earn.

FIRST STEPS IN THE THEATRE

Gilbert's first literary effort came about as the result of a commission to translate the Laughing Song from *Manon Lescaut* into English for Mme Parepa-Rosa, the wife of Carl Rosa, an opera impresario who founded a successful English touring opera company bearing his name. Gilbert later re-used the words in his "per-version" of Tennyson's *The Princess*. However, his first real success was with the magazine *Fun*, founded in 1861 and often called the "penny *Punch*", though it was more radical in outlook than its great contemporary. Gilbert submitted a short humorous article, illustrated with a line drawing. As a result, he was promptly engaged for life as a regular contributor under his pen-name "Bab", and his *Bab Ballads* became classics in their own right as did his accompanying vivacious, but often savage, caricatures. Even more important, they were a constant source of plots, dialogue and ideas.

At this time, Gilbert formed a society of cronies from the literary and theatrical world, called "The Serious Family", who used to meet for a meal at his lodgings. Amongst them was the dramatist Tom Robertson, who encouraged his host to write for the stage. So in December 1865 Gilbert's Christmas extravaganza, which positively bristled with puns, opened at the St James' theatre for two weeks. The following year his Christmas offering was a burlesque of Donizetti's *L'Elisir d'Amore*, called *Dulcamara*, with the dreadful subtitle of *The Little Duck or the Great Quack*, which Gilbert directed himself. His apprentice works were all burlesques, extravaganzas, pantomimes or parodies. He wrote a version of Meyerbeer's opera *Robert Le Diable* for John Hollingshead at the Gaiety theatre, which was soon to see the production of *Thespis*. From such inauspicious beginnings, he developed his extraordinary professionalism and theatrical sense.

*S*avoy stars pose for the camera in costume for two of a series of picture postcards.

In 1866, in his capacity as critic for *Fun*, Gilbert attended a performance of a one-act opera called *Cox and Box*, with a libretto by Burnand and music by the rising young star of serious musical composition, Arthur Sullivan. Gilbert's criticism was prophetic – while admiring the music, he felt that "the grand and graceful have, we think, too large a share of the honours to themselves". At this time, though Sullivan was an established figure in his own world, Gilbert was one of many hack London dramatists, and only unusual in that he, in common with the impresario German Reed, felt that the popular theatre could attract the crowds by offering its audiences good clean family fun, rather than sexual innuendo, or spectacular stage effects. In this, of course, he was to be proved right.

Gilbert's creativity increased; in 1871 at the Royal Court theatre alone he put on four plays in one year. Yet he still had time for his litigious nature to assert itself, erupting into frequent law-suits, and quarrels. In 1874 he quarrelled with the actress Henrietta Hodson, who had objected to his rudeness when she sat down heavily on the stage – "I always thought you would make an impression on the stage one day," commented Gilbert. The press admonished him: "Mr Gilbert has yet to learn that he is a servant of the public and amenable to public opinion."

A MAN OF CONTRADICTIONS

Such, at least, was Gilbert's public persona at this time. Yet, in 1867, this irascible, sharpspoken and impatient man had made what was to prove a very happy marriage to the gentle 17-year-old daughter of an army officer. Pretty, blonde and nicknamed affectionately, if somewhat patronisingly, by Gilbert as "Kitten", Lucy Turner was always the soul of tact and support, and was rewarded by Gilbert's undying love. His eyes were to stray occasionally, but there is no evidence that he was anything but physically faithful to her. They lived comfortably in Kensington for ten years, before Gilbert built Grim's Dyke, a splendid house in Harrow, complete with every modern domestic convenience. In its beautiful grounds, he constructed an artificial lake that looked far too peaceful to be the scene of his tragic death in May 1911.

An excellent sketch of Gilbert's appearance was given by the *New York Herald* in 1879, when he first visited America:

"He is a fine, well-made robust man, apparently forty-five, above the medium stature, with the brightest and rosiest of faces, an auburn moustache and short mutton-chop whiskers tipped only slightly with grey, large and clear blue eyes and a forehead of a high, massive and intellectual cast. His voice has a hearty deep ring and his utterance is quick and jerky – as though he were almost tired of this business of saying funny things which everybody more or less expects of him."

This perspicacious final comment was the theme not only of a *Bab Ballad*, Jester James, but also the dilemma which constantly faces Jack Point in *The Yeomen of the Guard*, for Gilbert did tire of the clown's role. His personality was in many ways more complex than that of Sullivan. Hyper-sensitive yet aggressive, he had a deep intolerance of pretence. For example, an eager Shakespearean scholar was disappointed to hear that Gilbert thought Shakespeare obscure. On being asked to give an example, Gilbert declaimed – "I would as lief be thrust through a quickset hedge as cry Pooh to a callow throstle". The scholar carefully explained the meaning of the phrase, but could not place its source; this was not surprising for Gilbert had invented it on the spur of the moment!

Whereas Sullivan, for all his apparent modesty, was a natural exhibitionist and performer, Gilbert was incredibly and gloomily nervous on first nights, and would absent himself until the final curtain when he would appear to take a bow. "What I suffered during those hours no man can tell. I have spent them at the club; I once went to a theatre alone to see a play; I have walked up and down the street; but no matter where I was, agony and apprehension possessed me."

Under his gruff exterior, Gilbert was an extremely kind man: he spent much money on the Bushey General Hospital near his home, and was always kind to the younger ladies of the chorus, when he had kept them rehearsing late, paying for cabs to take them home. He constantly visited the house of Clement Scott, one of his sternest critics, when Scott was ill, even though they had apparently been theatrical enemies. One of the best-known early Savoy stars, Jessie Bond, remembered the kindness he showed her when she had badly injured her ankle and could not dance. He wrote her a static serious song in *Iolanthe* so that she would not have to move – it was, of course, Iolanthe's plea for Strephon, "He loves". Deeply shy, yet engaged in the most extrovert of professions, constantly acid and wounding verbally, but kind in his actions, satirical yet sentimental, Gilbert was a walking example of his own topsy-turvydom.

THE SOCIALITE COMPOSER

Socially, Arthur Sullivan was more upwardly mobile than his future partner. Born in Lambeth at 8 Bolwell Terrace on 13 May 1842, he had a financially impoverished, but emotionally rich, childhood, in complete contrast to that of Gilbert. His warm-hearted parents both had Irish blood, while his mother was additionally of Italian and possibly Jewish extraction. Arthur and his brother Fred were joint apples of the parental eye, but Arthur was his father's shadow. He was precociously musical: his father, having been a clarinet player earning a guinea a week in the Surrey theatre, became more prosperous on joining the music staff of the Royal Military College at Sandhurst, and at the age of five Sullivan is reputed to have learnt to play all the military band instruments. Though he was sent

Though Gilbert was opposed to the star system, leading members of the company, such as George Grossmith (photographed here as Ko-Ko top), became household names. The leading ladies of the period (above) also attracted their quota of male admirers; the Prince of Wales was a fan of Jessie Bond.

away to boarding school at the age of eight, he soon begged to try for a chorister's place at the Chapel Royal. The principal, Thomas Helmore, was so impressed by the boy that he was accepted, although he was, at 12, somewhat old for admission. However, he was so talented that he soon became Head Chorister; his solo at the Duke of Albany's christening earnt him a royal pat on the head and, more importantly, a half sovereign from the Prince Consort. His friends among the select band of little boys included the Cellier brothers, Alfred and François, who were later to be very much part of Sullivan's life. He began composing regularly at this stage, and his anthem *O Israel* was published when he was only 13.

Sullivan's upward climb continued with the award of the first Mendelssohn scholarship to the Royal Academy of Music donated by the great Swedish soprano Jenny Lind and the upward climb began. The summit was to be friendship with the crowned heads of Europe, recognition as England's first great composer for over 200 years, and a prosperity which withstood the enormous inroads made upon his earnings by his huge gambling losses and an extravagantly hospitable way of life. His position was attained by charm, quick wits, an astute ability to be in the right place at the right time, and an almost Mozartian fluency and facility in composing the type of music loved by Victorian Britain. The price, however, was constant ill-health and pain from a chronic kidney condition, and a deep inner disappointment at his inability to write a great serious musical work.

FAMOUS OVERNIGHT

At 16 when his scholarship was extended to allow him to study in Leipzig, Sullivan was buoyant. By the time he was 20, he had become famous overnight. He had written some incidental music to *The Tempest* and his influential friend George Grove, who was secretary of the Crystal Palace concerts, arranged its performance. Taken up by the rich and fashionable and "shown about like a stuffed gorilla" according to his diary, he could nevertheless always laugh at himself. By 1866 he was writing a *Te Deum* for the Prince of Wales' wedding at Queen Victoria's command, and the Duke of Edinburgh had become a lifelong friend. In the same year a festival was devoted to his music, for which he wrote his *Irish Symphony*. One of his posts was organist to the Royal Italian Opera, where he was to learn much of his theatrical expertise; soon, he was asked by Francis Cowley Burnand (1836–1917) to set *Cox and Box*.

LIFE AT THE TOP

Naturally this charming and good-looking young man made a great impression on the ladies of his acquaintance, including Rachel Scott Russell, whom he met in 1863, and to whom he became unofficially

Gilbert, as seen in 1886 by Frank Hal, at home in his beloved Grim's Dyke. Despite outward appearances, he lacked confidence, as opposed to the self-possessed Sullivan.

engaged. Her family was intellectual and monied, her father both a Fellow of the Royal Society and a shipyard owner. Rachel was a very intense young lady – she believed that in Sullivan she had found a genius, and she was a determined Egeria. She begged him to write "a grand vigorous great work. Oh strain every nerve for my sake". But parental opposition to the match was enormous because of Sullivan's profligacy and consequent impecuniousness, and eventually the engagement was broken off in 1869. Rachel married and went to India with her civil servant husband.

Meanwhile, in 1867 Sullivan and Grove had made a major musicological discovery. Both had always loved Schubert and championed his music and they managed to unearth the missing parts of *Rosamunde* and the score of the C minor (Tragic) symphony in Vienna through the help of Schubert's nephew Schneider. At the same time, Sullivan's own compositional activity was increasing. He wrote the music for Burnand's *La Contrabandista* in 1867, while establishing himself as a major conductor and composer at the great provincial choral festivals. In 1866 he became a professor at the Royal Academy of Music and nine years later was the founding Principal of the National Training School for Music, which became the Royal College of Music. But in 1872 his life began to be darkened by a serious kidney complaint, which only was temporarily relieved by an operation to remove a kidney stone in 1879. Nevertheless he managed to travel abroad frequently, often in the company of the Duke of Edinburgh and Frederic Clay.

SULLIVAN'S "LITTLE WOMAN"

Sullivan's personal life was extremely satisfactory, too. In the 1870s the wealthy and beautiful Mrs Fanny Ronalds became his mistress. She was separated from her American husband and had the entrée, despite this, into many of society's most prestigious homes. A fine singer, she popularised Sullivan's ballad, *The Lost Chord* (the song's manuscript was buried with her). She was somewhat of a femme fatale (Lord Randolph Churchill was supposed to be in love with her at one time), and her house at 7 Cadogan Place became one of London's leading cultural salons. Ten years older than Sullivan, she became his hostess, adviser on social and even musical matters, and was in constant touch with him even when he was abroad. The epithet "L.W." (Little Woman) for this glittering and poised figure

A *company audition book. Gilbert was a tireless stage director and took great care over casting.*

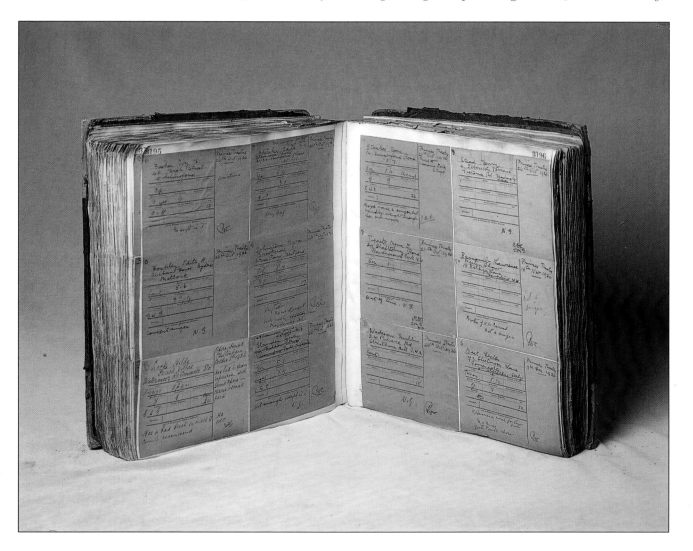

D'Oyly Carte
caricatured at the height
of his success with the
plans of the Savoy and his
Royal English Opera
House under his arm. The
latter was Carte's one ill-
judged venture; though
Sullivan's Ivanhoe was
initially a success, the
idea of a native school of
grand opera was
still-born. Sullivan
ruefully commented that
"the cobbler should stick
to his last" (above).

in Sullivan's diaries seems patronisingly inappropriate, especially when coupled with the (frequent) cryptic numbers which were his symbol for sexual intercourse. These meaningful numbers were often used to describe meetings with other "Little Women"! Sullivan was certainly sexually active and promiscuous throughout his adult life, in contrast with Gilbert's happily married faithfulness.

HONOURED BY THE QUEEN

Parallel with his successful partnership with Gilbert, Sullivan's eminence continued to grow in the world of creative music, culminating in his knighthood in 1883. In 1888 he performed his *The Golden Legend* at a Royal Command performance; the occasion elicited what was to prove a somewhat fatal suggestion from Queen Victoria: "You ought to write a grand opera, Sir Arthur; you would do it so well."

The *New York Herald* article of November 1879, which described Gilbert so vividly, also gives an equally clear picture of Sullivan:

"Gentle feeling and tender emotion are as strongly expressed, as cold glittering keen-edged intellect is in that of Mr Gilbert. He is short, round and plump with a very fleshy neck and as dark as his "collaborateur" is fair, with a face of wonderful mobility and sensitiveness in which the slightest emotion plays with unmistakeable meaning, with eyes which only the Germanic adjective of soulful would fully describe, and the full sensuous lips of a man of impassionate nature. With all this Mr Sullivan, who keeps a monocle dangling over one eye while the other twinkles merrily at you and whose dark whiskers and hair have an ambrosial curl, is something of a polished man of fashion."

Sullivan's charm, warmth and tact inspired the love of his many loyal friends, who were, however, drawn only from the ranks of the wealthy or famous, and any unselfishness tended to be limited to his family. Gilbert's unostentatious kindness extended to the lowest members of the company. The performer in Sullivan was always tuned to his audience and to his need for public approval, but Gilbert was unaware of the effect of his wounding tongue on more sensitive souls, and did not consider whether he was popular. Whereas Gilbert was always organized and worked like a long-distance runner, hard but well-paced, Sullivan was a sprinter, who could only produce when the adrenalin was high and there was an imminent deadline.

THE TWO MEN MEET

In November 1869 one of Sullivan's closest friends, the composer Frederic Clay took him to a rehearsal of Clay's new comic opera, *Ages Ago* at German Reed's "Gallery of Illustration", where *Cox and Box* had been produced three years previously; the librettist was W. S. Gilbert and the opera's ghostly subject was to be used again in *Ruddigore* 18 years later. Clay introduced Sullivan to Gilbert, who perversely tried to blind the composer with musical science, quoting a piece of nonsense from his comedy *The Palace of Truth*, asking Sullivan's opinion of the following: "When a musician who is master of many instruments has a musical theme to express, he can express it upon the simple tetrachord of Mercury (in which there are, as we all know, no diatonic intervals whatever) ..." and so on. Sullivan, probably rather irritated, said he would think about it!

No meeting could have been less auspicious – the practical, professional, but basically hack author with a chip on his shoulder, trying to impress the successful and glossy society darling.

THE ROLE OF D'OYLY CARTE

The man who was to forge the talents of these two disparate personalities into a creative sword that cut through the banality and parochialism of native English light opera, was christened Richard Doyle McCarthy and was born in Greek Street, Soho, on 3 May 1844. His father was a flautist, who owned an instrument-making company Rudall, Rose and Co, which later became the famous firm of Rudall Carte and was the first to import the saxophone into London. Richard invented a "new" flute, which is now in the Victoria and Albert Museum. Like Sullivan, he had Irish blood, and had a woodwind player for a father; indeed the two men became devoted friends. His mother, Eliza Jones, was the daughter of a cultivated and literary clergyman. She claimed French descent and made Richard speak French for two days a week at home. He was the eldest of six children and the whole family were creatively orientated: he mounted plays in a model theatre, which were so impressively atmospheric that a younger sister is reported to have burst into tears and vowed never to watch another production by her brother.

Carte went to University College School from 1856 to 1860, and, like Gilbert, proceeded to London University, but did not take his degree, deciding instead, after a year, to go into his father's business. By 1870, he had set himself up as a concert agent in Charing Cross Road with singers, dramatists and lecturers on his books, including the great Adelina Patti, the poet Matthew Arnold and Oscar Wilde. But he had always wanted to be an impresario, and became manager of the Royal Theatre, Soho, which specialized in operas and burlesques. Now, he was poised to fulfil his 1869 ambition, when he had stated that his life's aim was to establish "English comic opera in a theatre devoted to that alone".

His childhood creativity continued into adult life and he wrote several operettas, under the nom-de-plume Mark Lynne. He produced the first, *Dr. Ambrosias,* when only 24. It was reasonably

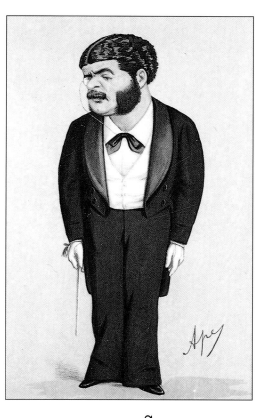

Sullivan, baton in hand, was caricatured by Spy (Leslie Ward) in 1874 in a cartoon entitled English music. Calm and carefree though Sullivan appeared on the surface, he suffered from ill-health, compounded by overwork and his tendency to compose in bursts right up to deadline (above).

Book 9 2428 4 Inch 13

Pellatt Cecile
Sandown
6 Knollys Rd Streatham SW

No professional
Experience
M E
Sent by Sims
Bull

Sept 16th 1913
R.D.C
F.C.

Voice.	Height.	Chorus or Parts.
Cont. Alto	above medium	Chorus
Quality of Voice.	Appearance.	Knowledge of Music.
	f9. to 9.21	f 9
Compass.	Salary Required.	Town.	Country.
B to G	=	✓	
Dialogue	} Has a lisp.		

LINE OF BUSINESS AND GENERAL REMARKS.
Has played Ruth Electa mchers & chorus of Pinafore Sings well useful Soprano Cont side   A R

useful chorus but probably not good enough else : too much for soubrette not big enough for heavy Contralto parts.

Kirkham Lilian   14 . IV
25 Humphrey St
Old Trafford
Manchester

Voice.	Height.	Chorus or Parts.
Cont.	Medium	Chorus.
Quality of Voice.	Appearance.	Knowledge of Music.
9.	f9. 26	f9.
Compass.	Salary Required.	Town.	Country.
9 to 7.	✓	✓	✓
Dialogue			

LINE OF BUSINESS AND GENERAL REMARKS.
Knows Chorus of Yeoman & Mikado. Is not wanting work at present. Good voice but rather muffled in places.   A R.

Crutchley Violet   14 . V 13.
611 Stockport Road
Longsight Manchester

Voice.	Height.	Chorus or Parts.
Sop.	Short.	Chorus
Quality of Voice.	Appearance.	Knowledge of Music.
9 . light.	f9. 23	f9
Compass.	Salary Required.	Town.	Country.
B to C	✓	✓	—
Dialogue	} Reads fairly	J. M. G.	

LINE OF BUSINESS AND GENERAL REMARKS.
pretty voice very light no stage experience.
A R.

Taylor. Mabel   14 . IV
4 Mella Grove
Bolton.

Voice.	Height.	Chorus or Parts.
Sop.	Medium	Chorus.
Quality of Voice.	Appearance.	Knowledge of Music.
9 to 9	f9. 20	f9.
Compass.	Salary Required.	Town.	Country.
B to B.	✓	✓	✓
Dialogue	}		

LINE OF BUSINESS AND GENERAL REMARKS.
Knows chorus of Patience most pleasant voice but plain perhaps will soften as she gets older   A R

Hope Phyllis
61 Manchester Rd
Bolton

Voice.	Height.	Chorus or Parts.
Sop.	Short	Chorus.
Quality of Voice.	Appearance.	Knowledge of Music.
f9 to 9	9. 20	f9.
Compass.	Salary Required.	Town.	Country.
C to C	✓	✓	—
Dialogue	}		

LINE OF BUSINESS AND GENERAL REMARKS.
Has only been in Pantomime very light voice pleasant quality.
A R.

successful. *Marie* followed at the Opera Comique in 1871, the same year as *Thespis,* and his last work at the Royalty in 1877 was called *Happy Hampstead.* By 1871 he was married to Blanche Prowse, whose father was one of the founders of Keith Prowse, but she died ten years later, leaving him with two sons, Lucas, who became a barrister, and Rupert, born in 1876, who was to succeed his father in the management of his opera company.

TOWARDS THE SAVOY

By 1875, Carte's office in Craig's Court off Shaftesbury Avenue was humming with the energy of this dapper little man with his "round dark eyes, a handsome well-chiselled face and a certain air of distinction and chic". His self-confidence may have not been deep, however, as a contemporary reported that he had a stutter. He possessed a slight physical resemblance to Sullivan, had the same impulsive intuitive nature, and worked with the same incredible energy in very short bursts, which needed a balance of equally energetic recreation; their mutual understanding must have been a strong factor in their friendship. Gilbert was never to be more than a respected colleague to either man.

In 1976, with a view to making his dream of a national English comic opera school a reality, and after the successful transference of *Trial by Jury* to the Opera Comique, Carte formed a syndicate called the Comedy Opera Company. Its directors were Tom Chappell and George Metzler (both music publishers), Augustus Drake Collard of the piano firm and Edward Hodgson Bailey, who had a virtual monopoly of cleaning the London streets with his wagons – hence his Dylan Thomas-type nickname, "Watercart Bailey". Each put up £500 and the capital was £6, 000. At first Michael Gunn, an Irish music publisher, was also a member, but he was sacked by the rest of the syndicate after he had been left in charge during Carte's absence in America with the *Pinafore* tour.

At this stage, however, neither Gilbert or Sullivan were directors, and Carte was appointed merely secretary and adviser. In their original agreement, made in June 1877, librettist and composer had promised that they would write their first full-length opera for the opera company for an advance fee of 200 guineas, to be paid on delivery of the completed work, and each would receive £6 royalty for each performance. So, the future was by no means predetermined. During the first uncertain years, Carte remained constantly visionary and optimistic, whereas the syndicate were edgy and cautious. They sent a telegram forbidding Carte's inspired engagement of the company's future star George Grossmith, they often gave members of the cast notice, but retracted it when box office receipts rose, they wanted to reduce Gilbert and Sullivan's share of the advance during the creation of *HMS Pinafore* and begged Carte to take it off during its slow beginning. Finally they tried to

These chorus audition notes show how the high standards Gilbert set became a company tradition. The complete books (inset) are still preserved.

ruin the performance of *Pinafore* on the night of the expiry of the Opera-Comique's lease. Carte was later to justifiably remind Gilbert and Sullivan that he had "stuck to it through thick and thin ... I incurred all the preliminary expenses at my own risk".

By the time of *The Pirates of Penzance,* Carte's determination and far-sightedness had launched all three men on an international career, and the members of the company themselves felt that they were a close-knit family and part of a "home of English talent", according to the singer Rutland Barrington. During the run of *Patience,* the company moved in 1881 to its final home – the Savoy Theatre. Purpose-built by Carte for the company, it gave the operas the name by which they are still known today. Carte later followed the theatre with the Savoy Hotel, renowned equally for its luxury, cuisine and decor.

On 8 February 1881, the final form of the D'Oyly Carte Opera Company took shape in a five-year agreement, in which Carte was granted the performing licence of all the Gilbert and Sullivan operas, each partner receiving a third of the profits from the enterprise after deduction of £4,000 a year rent for the theatre, and all necessary expenses including "repairs incidental to the performance". In these last innocuous words lay the seed of the fierce quarrel that later was to shatter the partnership. Though Gilbert and Sullivan had a veto on engagement of artists, and engaged all principals and controlled the rehearsals, Carte held the preliminary auditions and those for chorus and understudies, managed the daily business of the theatre, salaries, advertising and purchase of stage equipment and master-minded the increasingly frequent tours.

Punch, for one, recognized D'Oyly Carte's importance in the partnership in this 1882 cartoon. Sullivan struck up a close relationship with Carte, but the prickly Gilbert often felt an outsider.

ENTER HELEN D'OYLY CARTE

All these achievements had the immeasurable support of one woman, Helen Lenoir. The daughter of the Procurator-Fiscal of Wigtown, her prosaic, but true, name was Susan Black, which she at first altered to Helen Susan Black when she went to London University. She obtained the General Certificate for Women (Honours Division) in 1871, the Special Certificate in Mathematics in 1873 and the Special Certificate in Logic and Moral Philosophy in 1874. At this time it was not possible for a woman to be awarded a traditional degree. She embarked on a career as actress and teacher before joining the administrative staff of the D'Oyly Carte company in 1877 as Helen Lenoir. She apparently lied about her age, but her date of birth has now been established as 12 May 1852.

Helen soon demonstrated her acumen and inventiveness in arranging the first hasty British performance of *The Pirates of Penzance* to establish copyright. She became more and more indispensable in running the increasingly complicated affairs of the tours, eventually ending up in the USA for six years in charge of all D'Oyly Carte affairs. A fine negotiator – her tactful handling of the

diverse personalities in the partnership was masterly – she was the obvious choice for Carte as his second wife, and Sullivan was delighted to be best man at their marriage in 1888. Thereafter, she was to be as active in the running of the Savoy Hotel as in the opera company, and presided graciously over the fashionable dinner parties held at her husband's house at 4 Adelphi Terrace, with its resplendent billiard room decorated by Whistler. George Edwardes, Carte's general manager for many years and later to be in charge of the Gaiety theatre, maintained that "the whole fabric of the Gilbert and Sullivan business rested on Miss Lenoir's shoulders". Though this may have been an exaggeration, it is certain that her diplomacy and practical calm were invaluable as a foil to Carte's inspiration and flair.

MUTUAL ADMIRATION

"Their partnership broken in life remains unbreakable in history," said Allardyce Nicholl of Gilbert and Sullivan. Both men valued and respected each other's professionalism. Gilbert's postcard of 19

Author, Composer, and "the harmless necessary Carte."—*Shakspeare.*

The contrary view to that of the Punch cartoon, shown on the previous pages. The depiction of Sullivan as a street hurdy-gurdy player is apt; by the end of each Savoy run, his 'melodies' had been 'dinned into our heads by every street organist', the young George Bernard Shaw ruefully reported.

November 1903 to François Cellier mourns that "A Gilbert is of no use without a Sullivan". He recognized that they both shared the same sense of humour: "When I tell him a joke he understand immediately. I never have to tell it twice, which is fatal." Both were born parodists and disliked artistic bombast and pretence; therefore the music's parody of pompous and grandiose styles enhanced the verbal tilting at the self-importance of many British institutions. Though Gilbert averred he had no musical ear and only knew two tunes – "One is God Save the Queen and one isn't" – his subtle sense of metre and rhythm must have been a constant inspiration. Sullivan was clearly aware of this, when he described the *Pirates'* libretto to his mother as "wonderfully funny . . . sometimes brilliant in dialogue – beautifully written for music, as in all Gilbert does." Both were aware of each other's problems and, despite Gilbert's volatile reactions to criticism, both were able to compromise. When Sullivan was having difficulty in setting Act II of *Utopia Limited*, Gilbert offered to add his words after the music was written, in the manner of the old burlesque style, even though the result was doggerel as he had feared. The mutual adulation of their messages to each other after the premiere of *The Gondoliers* sums up their appreciation of each other's gifts. Gilbert speaks first:

"I must thank you for all the magnificent work you have put into the piece. It gives one the chance of shining right through the twentieth century with a reflected light." Sullivan responded:

"Don't talk of reflected light. In such a perfect book as *The Gondoliers* you shine with an individual brilliancy which no other writer can hope to attain."

THE RIFT IN THE LUTE

If only it had ended there – but the rest, if not silence, was bathos. After the failure of *The Grand Duke,* they appeared together to take a curtain call at a revival of *The Sorcerer* and *Trial by Jury.* On opposite sides of the stage, they were fortunately separated by Carte, but the audience must have noticed each man's studious disregard of the other's presence and the lack of congratulatory handshakes. The main reason for this was a series of quarrels, but the real roots of their differences lay far deeper.

Both men had come from very different backgrounds – Gilbert had not known poverty in a solidly middle-class childhood, but had a struggle to earn a living as a young man. Sullivan's parents were genuinely poor in his early childhood, but though not rich in his twenties, he had received early recognition and financial reward. His social advancement was staggeringly fast, whereas Gilbert never wanted to be a society lion and probably was not envious of Sullivan's exotic life-style and hob-nobbing with royalty.

But in every other way Gilbert was jealous and resentful of Sullivan. He was certainly jealous of Sullivan's friendship with Carte and his sense of exclusion, especially when Sullivan was Carte's best man at his wedding to Helen, may have exacerbated his fury when Sullivan would not side with him against Carte at the time of the celebrated carpet quarrel. Throughout his life Gilbert looked for insults and slights, which he would often take to court to settle. Sullivan was far more tolerant, easy-going and secure in his personal and professional relationships.

In addition to personal envy, Gilbert was resentful of the critical reaction to the operas. Almost invariably the music was praised, but if any fault was found, it was with the text. Sullivan, on the other hand, must have disliked the habitual use of Gilbert's name in front of his on the Savoy programmes. Gilbert felt that there was, as in *Ruddigore,* simply too much music of too high a quality, which would deflect attention from the libretto. In a *Mikado* rehearsal, he told Nanki-Poo, "There are one or two words which fail to reach me quite distinctly. Sullivan's music is of course very beautiful and I heard every note without difficulty, but I think my words are not altogether without merit". His determination that his words should be fully appreciated led to his printing of the libretto for the audience to follow, but, no doubt, Sullivan felt that the constant rustling of pages detracted equally from the beauty of his music. The final confirmation of his sense of inferiority must have been the public recognition of Sullivan's services to music by a knighthood, when none was offered to Gilbert.

Though Gilbert did not neglect his other theatrical work, he was not distracted by the demands of a different and more serious form of his art. Sullivan had to resist the pressure from the critics and even from royalty to abandon the frivolity of the Savoy operas and devote himself to serious works, preferably choral and religious, as fodder for the voracious choirs of the big provincial festivals. This lure led Sullivan to protest constantly against the artificiality of Gilbert's plots, and to long for more human emotions and aspirations to express musically.

D'Oyly Carte was known unkindly as "Oily" Carte because of his famous tact. But it was certainly all needed to extract what he wanted from his joint goldmine, and to balance their talents so that he could establish his school of national comic opera, with Gilbert and Sullivan operas as its pivots. He sympathised with Sullivan's dislike of artificiality and longing for more lyricism, in that he wanted to abolish French frivolity and to pursue the aims of opéra-comique rather than opéra-bouffe. But in 1906, Gilbert himself stressed in a speech that all three of them were determined that "our plots, however ridiculous, should be coherent, that our dialogue should be void of offence: that on artistic principles, no man should play a woman's part and no woman a man's. Finally we agreed that no lady of the company should be expected to wear a dress that she could not wear with absolute propriety at a private fancy-dress ball".

Carte had the vision to see in *Thespis* the possibilities of mutual inspiration in the partnership, and the courage to back his hunch. Thereafter, during the quarrels of the late 1880s onwards, he constantly tried to make each man see the other's point of view. He appreciated their humour, and was in fact witty himself. Queen Victoria at the command performance of *The Gondoliers*, asked Carte why there were so many interpolations into the text. The *Era* of 14 March 1891 reported Carte's reply:

"'These, your Majesty,' said Carte, 'are what we call gags.'

'Gags?' replied the Queen, 'I thought gags were things that were put by authority into people's mouths.'

'These gags, your Majesty,' answered the manager, bowing profoundly, 'are things that people put into their own mouths without authority.'

The Queen smiled benignly and seemed perfectly satisfied with the ready reply."

His business acumen and flair for publicity boosted the operas

Members of the company recorded the dates of their first appearance in this autograph book. Among the famous names here are Julia Gwynne, whose career started at the Opera Comique, Jessie Bond (1881) and Bertha Lewis (1909).

Performed in Gilbert and Sullivan Operas at the Old Savoy or earlier

Signature	First Appearance	Signature	First Appearance
Julia Gwynne (Mrs George Edwardes)	(Opera Comique) 1878	Nelly Bromley (Mrs Archibald Stuart Wortley)	1875
Leonora Braham	1881	W. R. Shirley	1888
Durward Lely	1881 (Opera Comique)	J. M. Gordon (on tour 1888)	1884
Jessie Bond	1878	Louie René	1894
Nancy McIntosh	1893	Scott Russell	1893
Henry A. Lytton	1885	Lillian Carr	1882
Marie Henri	1885	Louie Pounds	1901
Braham Ulmar	1881	Cissie Saumarez (Mrs Arthur Whitby)	1889
M. Forbes Rice	1881 (Opera Comique)	Walter Passmore	1893
Sibyl Grey	1878	Agnes Fraser	1900
Les Rofford	1907	Avey Clayards	1884
Bertha Lewis	1909	Decima Moore	1889
Sydney Granville	1907	Neva Bond	1880
Georgie Sinclair	1887	John Coates	1893
Ella S. Nelson	1892	Jennie Sullivan	1877
Ernest Blackford	1893	Madame Gaston	1891
Frank H. Crimp	1894	Jeffrey T. Snelson	1893
E. A. Fleming	(Opera Comique) 1877	Charles Stuart	1891
Annie Bernard	1883	Allen Morris	1881
Clara Dow	1907	J. R. Blake Johnston	1889
Blanche Gaston-Murray	1877	Tiny Murray	1882
Harry Stratton	1878	Strafford Moss	1897
Ethel Jeffreys	1889	Jessie Cortie Pounds	1882
Richard Anderson	1906	Kate Chard	1883

on many an occasion. First nights were notable for his strategic placing of personalities featured in the operas in prominent stall seats, as Wilde in *Patience* or Captain Shaw in *Iolanthe*. His clever, but constant, battle against pirating of music or words reached an amusingly ingenious climax when, having heard of the intention of Mr Duff, an American theatre manager, to pirate *The Mikado*, Carte spirited the whole company over the Atlantic under assumed names and on a different ship from the one on which they were expected to sail. They opened successfully in New York before their rival. Without Carte, as mediator and entrepreneur, it is possible that the storms that arose from the confrontation of Gilbert's irascibility and jealousy with Sullivan's lack of commitment to comic opera and dislike of so many of the proffered plots might have wrecked the Savoy ship. As it was, he used the temporary calm between disagreements as a fresh inspiration for their most popular works, *The Mikado* and *The Gondoliers*.

CHAPTER THREE

WORDS
AND
MUSIC

I T IS OFTEN FORGOTTEN that Gilbert's stage plays formed the bulk of his output and provided him with much of his income. Many were in blank verse (*Rosencrantz and Guildenstern, Pygmalion and Galatea, The Princess, Gretchen,* and his favourite *Broken Hearts*), some were "fairy" plays (*Foggerty's Fairy, The Wicked World, The Palace of Truth*), others were prose dramas (*Dan'l Druce*) and usually of a saccharinely sentimental nature. He dipped into them for material for the Savoy operas, but regarded them as his serious work. The bubblingly inventive source of his plots and texts was the *Bab Ballads,* effortlessly churned out for *Fun* from 1861–1879, with their calculated and sophisticated language often full of puns and double-entendres, and adorned with his quirkily individual satiric drawings that had a savagery that was absent from his verbal humour.

The style of all the Savoy texts is drawn from the *Bab Ballads:* often, whole poems are transposed unaltered into the operas, as in the case of "The Darned Mounseer", "The Highly Respectable Gondolier", and many of the biographical and patter songs. The stories, too, of many of the *Ballads,* have a surrealistic side that expanded well into Gilbert's own zanily logical "all-change" final solutions to his convoluted plots.

GILBERTIAN RHYME AND RHYTHM

Gilbert's serious lyrics are not usually very individual, being typical of the style of the era rather than the writer, though the best have been flatteringly likened to Herrick. It is in the realms of parody and satire that he is at his most inspired: Meredith summed up his gifts when writing his memorial inscription "His foe was folly and his weapon wit." The Gilbertian style is easily recognizable, being compounded of a rhyming inventiveness worthy of Ogden Nash, and a love of internal rhyme – that is within, as well as at the end of a line. Dazzlingly varied metres and rhythms immediately suggest their musical counterpart, and the occasional pun leavens the mix: the famous "are men, but 'Are Men' stuck in her throat" in *Princess Ida* presupposed an almost academic knowledge of *Macbeth* in his audience, who had been more used to the groaning Planché-type pun "Walking this forest long, I long for rest". However, they no doubt enjoyed the creak of Gama's answer to the query of whether there were "no males whatever in those walls" – "None, gentlemen, excepting letter mails".

The sheer brilliance of language tended to increase throughout the Savoy operas, possibly achieving its most consistent level in *Patience,* but becoming its own sterile enemy in *Utopia Limited* and *The Grand Duke,* when self-indulgent word-spinning destroyed any theatrical sense. There are several types of rhyming techniques that Gilbert uses. The internal rhyme tends to occur most in the patter songs: "to fit the wit of a bit of a chit" in Hildebrand's song

*I*sadore Godfrey was music director of the D'Oyly Carte Opera Company from 1929 to 1968. Godfrey served the company faithfully over the years until his eventual retirement; his recordings of the Gilbert and Sullivan operas still stand as the authentic standard (above).

(*Princess Ida*, Act II) or Bunthorne's "You must lie upon the daisies and discourse in novel phrases" in *Patience* are typical examples. Sometimes he combines internal rhymes with onomatopoeia as in the opening lines of "When the night wind howls in the chimney cowls", the opening lines of Sir Roderic's song in *Ruddigore*. He enjoyed making up words as in "pottery-terra-cottery-lottery" in *Patience,* and in distortion to fit a rhyme – "nussed" (instead of nursed) and "crust" in *HMS Pinafore,* and the notorious "lowest" and "ghoest" in *The Grand Duke.* Proper names are used as part of a rhyming scheme, as in Hannibal and "cannibal" (*Patience*), Phoebe and "She be" *(The Yeomen of the Guard),* Pinafore and "din afore" *(The Pirates of Penzance),* and Cranberry and Banbury *(Iolanthe).* He tends to fall back on the repetition of final words of lines – "not so", "jot so", "plot so" and "got so" in *The Pirates of Penzance,* for example. Some of the most amusing examples are two or even three words rhymed with single words.

There is infinite variety in Gilbert's rhythmic sense, metre and constant use of irregular line lengths. A good example, that paid musical dividends, is the Gama's sons' trio in Act II of *Princess Ida,* where the comically short lines at "Dismay us" and "He'll slay us" have a stolid stupidity, which evoked a very funny musical setting from Sullivan. Leila and Fleta's charming "Don't go" in *Iolanthe,* the interesting line lengths in Alexis' ballad "Love Feeds" in *The Sorcerer,* the marvellous gallop of so many of the patter songs, as in *Patience* – "A steady and stolidly, jolly bank holiday Every-day young man" – or "Bright little, tight little, slight little, light little, trim little, prim little craft" *(Ruddigore),* all cry out for music. He often uses alliteration – one of the most telling examples being the "song of a merryman, moping mum" in *The Yeomen of the Guard* duet between Elsie Maynard and Jack Point, or the "every-day young girls" who are "prettily pattering, cheerily chattering" in *Patience.* A deliberate use of long stresses helps create a comic atmosphere, as in the deliberately bombastic "With cat-like tread Upon our prey we steal" of the pirate chorus in Act II of *The Pirates of Penzance.* A lightness and subtlety is indicated by his use of feminine-ending syllables, as in Nanki-Poo's "Through every passion ranging And to your humours changing", which all add to the appeal of his "supple song". Despite his constant declaration that he was unmusical, Gilbert was more rhythmically aware than many professional musicians, whether deliberately creating a perfect gavotte measure in "I am a courtier grave and serious" (Act II, *The Gondoliers*), or more generally in his tumbling rhythms.

The company's longest serving music director retires. One of Godfrey's last productions was a long-awaited revival of Utopia Limited.

GILBERTIAN DIALOGUE AND PLOT

The style of Gilbert's dialogue was less successful. Audiences generally feel that it has to be "got through" to further the story, and usher in the next song or ensemble. Whereas the verse seems eternal in its wit, the dialogue now appears heavy, over-complex and at best quaintly stylised. In fact, much of it resembles the texts of Gilbert's plays, and, as such, it is understandable that the latter have not survived. Gilbert needed the thought of a musical setting just as much as Sullivan needed the inspiration of Gilbert's felicitous verses to produce memorable music. Otherwise both men became verbally or musically platitudinous and dull.

However, the social allusions were always to the point, as were Gilbert's parodistic view of the follies of the law, politics, ambition, or artistic pretence, which form the backbone of so many of the operas. The constant minor contemporary references tend to need an explanatory glossary today, as in Colonel Calverley's Act I song in *Patience*, but Gilbert's attack on more general targets is as relevant today as it was a century ago. We can still laugh at the law in *Trial by Jury* and *Iolanthe*, the navy and the army in *HMS Pinafore* and *The Pirates of Penzance* respectively, mindless cult adoration in *Patience*, the more excessive characteristics of Women's Lib. in *Princess Ida*, the inefficiency of the House of Lords in *Iolanthe*, petty officialdom in *The Mikado*, the popular melodrama in *Ruddigore*, and British politics and jingoism in *Utopia Limited*. The idea of limited companies was attacked there too, as it had

Recording Gilbert and Sullivan in 1962. The D'Oyly Carte Company had first ventured into the recording studio in the 1920s, but now things were very different. Note the marked squares on which the principal singers are standing; these were used to give the records a stage atmosphere by recreating the theatrical moves.

been in *The Gondoliers*. Only *The Yeoman of the Guard* is free from any specified butt. In the case of jingoism and patriotism, the mockery is gentle: there is something lovable in the the pirates' meek capitulation at the sight of the Union Jack – after all, they are "all noblemen who have gone wrong" – and the aggressive patriotism of "For he is an Englishman" in *HMS Pinafore* is surely sincere.

Gilbert's mockery lay not only in the plot ingredients, but also in the use of parody (though to a lesser extent than Sullivan) by parody. He constantly mocks the verbose and the pretentious in the law by imitating its language, notably in *Trial by Jury* and *Iolanthe*. In *Patience,* too, the intense, passionate and despairing style of Swinburne is hilariously caught in Bunthorne's poem "Hollow! Hollow! Hollow!" as well as the verbal clichés of the artistic intelligentsia of the time.

GILBERT AND WOMEN

There has been much comment on Gilbert's attitude to middle-aged women. His first reference to them is in *Trial by Jury*, when the Judge tells us how he "threw over" a rich attorney's "elderly

Behind the scenes at the company's costume and scenery store. The main picture is of the binnacle of HMS Pinafore; the skips (inset) show just how much was involved in keeping D'Oyly Carte on the road.

ugly daughter" who "may very well pass for 43 in the dusk with the light behind her". Chronologically, the portraits tend to become steadily crueller, but also more fleshed out in every sense of the word. *The Sorcerer*'s Lady Sangazure is touching rather than laughable in her reticent love for Sir Marmaduke. Little Buttercup's love for Captain Corcoran in *HMS Pinafore* is eventually requited, and she is described as rosy and round or plump and pleasing, so she is by no means unattractive. But Ruth, the pirate maid-of-all-work in *The Pirates of Penzance*, with her dishonesty and embarrassing love for a man half her age, was to become a Gilbertian stereotype. Lady Jane, like Ruth, loves someone who does not love her, but her dogged devotion to Bunthorne elicits a certain admiration, as does the dignified, but inappropriate, love of the Queen of the Fairies for Private Willis. In *Princess Ida*'s Lady Blanche, there is a hardness and ambition which is only re-encountered in *The Mikado*'s Katisha, but, unlike the latter, there is no pathos in her, merely humourless pretentiousness. Her only redeeming trait is her affection for her daughter Melissa.

With Katisha, the apogee of Gilbert's hatred and even fear of the power of middle-aged ladies is reached. Even her occasional lapses into pathos are only momentary, and her bloodthirstiness and engulfing of her hapless mate Ko-Ko are similar to that of a large female spider devouring its mate. After Katisha, Dame Hannah

R*ecording The Yeomen of the Guard in 1964, principals in the foreground, chorus in the background. Note, too, how the orchestra layout has changed, with the conductor immediately in front of the stage and the orchestra behind him (left).*

in *Ruddigore* and Dame Carruthers in *The Yeoman of the Guard* are harmless and pleasant: it is not until *The Gondoliers* that another man-eating dragon appears in the Duchess of Plaza-Toro. Understandably, during the writing of *Utopia Limited*, Sullivan was begging Gilbert not to produce yet another fearsome female, but a "dignified, stately, well made-up and well dressed lady" who would be "a charming feature in a piece". Indeed, Lady Sophy is a pleasant and comparatively believable creation, if a little lifeless and wan. But the Baroness von Krakenfeldt in *The Grand Duke* is a sawdust version of her forbears and wearily ineffectual as either a figure of fun or evoker of fear.

Nobody has conclusively analysed the reason behind Gilbert's creation of these characters. They can be explained away as pantomime dames, but they are more powerful and dislikeable in their strongest form. Perhaps Gilbert's unhappy relationship with his cold, hard mother and his sense of being overwhelmed by his older sisters led to his obsession.

C*ostumes from the operas in store; a Mikado kimono features prominently. Costume notes and fabric swatches are seen on the left.*

His attitude to women was that of a typical chauvinist. In *Princess Ida*, though he makes his heroine brave and intelligent, he also makes her determination comic and pointless, in that she finally has to admit feminine weakness. He clearly sees all female learning and indeed emancipation as something about which his own Kitten clearly would not have bothered her pretty little head! Otherwise his heroines are often either snobbish, like Josephine or Mabel, or conceited like Yum-Yum, or Julia Jellicoe. However Phyllis, Patience and Phoebe possess a certain simple practicality, while Elsie Maynard has courage. Gilbert's general attitude is that women must be young, pretty and preferably either mindlessly in love, flirtatiously unattainable, or, like Rose in *Ruddigore*, fundamentally disloyal. It is strange that in his maturer years he surrounded himself with young girls.

THE IDEA OF TOPSY-TURVYDOM

All Gilbert's plots hinge on coincidence, accident or birth, class-consciousness, the triumph of young love, and the often over-neat sorting out of couples. Even the semi-tragic *Yeomen* almost fits this mould. The use of role reversal, and of the appearance being different from actuality, made Gilbert coin the word "Topsy-turvydom" to describe the nature of these themes. He wrote:

> I dreamt that somehow I had come
> To dwell in topsy-turvydom
> Where vice is virtue – virtue vice
> Where nice is nasty – nasty nice:
> Where right is wrong and wrong is right
> Where white is black and black is white."

He tends to upset all social mores to side with those who rebel, and yet in the end, all reverts to an established pattern, and the rebels are shown to be unpractical idealists. In *HMS Pinafore*, the putative lovers are alternately eligible or non-eligible according to the

*G*odfrey was noted for his clear beat and his ability to keep stage and pit together – a vital quality when faced with short rehearsal periods and mixed touring conditions. Here, he prepares to launch a recording session (above).

*G*odfrey photographed with Sir Malcolm Sargent, another great Savoyard. Sargent was a guest conductor in the 1920s and directed the company's first recordings. He returned after the Second World War and in 1961.

class to which they rightfully belong. The heroes of *The Gondoliers* cannot remain republican kings, but revert to their natural status, while Rose's affections in *Ruddigore* wax and wane with the social fortunes of her lovers. In the topsy-turvy world, however violent the reversals of the natural order, the status quo is always finally restored. George Bernard Shaw found this most irritating:

"Paradoxical wit, astonishing to the ordinary Englishman, is nothing to me. Nature has cursed me with a facility for the same trick: and I could paradox Mr Gilbert's head off if I were convinced that such trifling is morally justifiable." Elsewhere: "He could always see beneath the surface of things; and if he could not have seen through them, he might have made his mark as a serious dramatist, instead of having, as a satirist, to depend for the piquancy of his ridicule on the general assumption of the validity of the very things he ridiculed. The theme of *The Pirates of Penzance* is essentially the same as that of Ibsen's *Wild Duck*".

GILBERT AT WORK

Gilbert's method of work was invariable. He rewrote the story-line about a dozen times and then read it to Sullivan, whose suggestions he often incorporated. The dialogue followed, thus establishing the outline of the action, before the skeleton was filled out with the songs. The first act was then sent to Sullivan to set to music while Gilbert wrote the lyrics for the second act. Only then did he add jokes in the dialogue, placing them very carefully. One of the tools he constantly tried to use to facilitate instant topsy-turvydom, was his so-called "Magic Lozenge" plot. This stemmed from folk-lore and was certainly in evidence in operas such as *L'Elisir d'Amore*, while Shakespeare even used a version of it in *A Midsummer Night's Dream*. Gilbert used it for the first time in *The Sorcerer*. On taking the magic lozenge, or, in *The Sorcerer*'s case, a love philtre, people either became the opposite of their actual character, or their feelings were turned upside-down. Gilbert kept proffering this idea like a hopeful puppy whenever a new libretto was required. Presented after *Iolanthe*, it reappeared both before and after *The Mikado;* on each occasion it was firmly rejected by Sullivan as silly, though Gilbert eventually used it in a musical context with Cellier in *The Mountebanks* in 1892 and with Edward German in *Fallen Fairies* in 1909.

A GIFTED STAGE DIRECTOR

Though Gilbert's verbal talent is still appreciated today, his equally great talent for stage-direction is often forgotten. Despite his bad-temper, he was loved by the company, ruling them like a benevolent despot. His determination to keep the sexes apart back-stage and to protect his actresses from too ardent admirers, earned the

Sargent in action in the recording studio, conducting The Yeomen of the Guard. His unique gift was his ability to reveal many of the felicities hidden in Sullivan's orchestration, helped by his study of the closely-guarded full scores.

The Fairy Queen's Wagnerian helmet, perched on a dummy, looks somewhat forelorn in this behind-the-scenes shot.

company the nickname of the Savoy boarding school! Gilbert insisted that his actors should believe in the sincerity of their words and actions, thus heightening, rather than diminishing, the text's humour. He pointed out that "directly the actors show that they are conscious of the absurdity of their utterances, the piece begins to drag", adding that "grimaces are derogatory to the comic actor's art" and "there must be no exaggeration in costume, make-up or demeanour". He trained his actors by discussing each character with them, which was quite a new procedure in those days of haphazard direction, and often let their suggestions add substance to the part. His ability was recognized in America, where the *New York Tribune* said "He was a tyrant at rehearsals", and "it would be better for the English stage if more English authors had a knowledge and authority equal to his".

He tried to get away from the star system, but paradoxically the strong personalities of his leading players all created a tradition of acting which continued after his death. He even introduced fines for "inappropriate, exaggerated or unauthorised business" and told Rutland Barrington, the original Guiseppe in *The Gondoliers,* that his part "must be played exactly as I wrote it".

Gilbert worked out his stage moves in advance, using three inch pieces of striped wood for the men, and two-and-a-half inch pieces for the women, coloured according to the differing pitch of their voices. He planned their movements, and those of the chorus on a miniature stage. His eye for detail was extraordinarily keen – he hated changes to the characters' appearance; when one of the chorus of peers shaved off his moustache while playing in *Iolanthe,* he promptly sacked him. All uniforms, state robes and stage scenes were absolutely realistic and exact down to the smallest detail.

Gilbert described his friend and mentor Tom Robertson, from whom he learnt so much, as "an exceedingly skilful dramatic tailor ... he fitted each character with the utmost nicety to the man or woman who was to play in it; and he was there to instruct them in every moment, every emphasis ... he invented stage-management ... showed how to give life and variety and nature to the scene by breaking it up with all sorts of little incidents and delicate by-play. I have been at many of his rehearsals and learnt a great deal from them". He could have been describing himself.

THE MUSIC OF THE OPERAS

Before his first collaboration with Gilbert on *Thespis,* Sullivan had written two light operas, *Cox and Box* (1866), which is still performed today, and in 1867, *La Contrabandista.* Both were successful in their day, but, compared to the Savoy operas, Sullivan's music seems slight and derivative. The same can be said of his serious output, where portentous solemnity is coupled with a lack of a distinctive personal style. What he wrote had an immediate appeal

for a contemporary audience, but now the majority of his classical compositions have been relegated to obscurity. His one grand opera, *Ivanhoe,* has sunk with little trace apart from a couple of songs, while the occasional performances of *The Golden Legend, The Prodigal Son,* the *Te Deum* or the *Martyr of Antioch* have resulted in hurried and embarrassed replacement of the scores on dusty library shelves: they have moments, intended in all serious-ness, that are disconcertingly close to some of Sullivan's parodies of other composers' music.

Gilbert's texts, however, seem to awake an inventiveness not to be found elsewhere, and a development of a personal Sullivanesque style. One of the most recognizable traits in the scores of the operas is an attractive irregularity of rhythm and stress, as in the elonga-tion of phrase-lengths in the first chorus of *Iolanthe,* or in the almost Carmen-like crowd music at the "Man of jollity" entry of Jack Point and Elsie Maynard in *The Yeomen of the Guard,* or the shifting of stress to half a beat backwards, as in "And O my darling O my pet" in *The Gondoliers.* Sullivan often followed the 18th-

A *Yeomen of the Guard play-back. Standing next to Sargent is John Reed, the Jack Point of the recording and one of the greatest exponents of the operas' patter roles (above).*

century practice of turning two bars of 3/4 into one bar of 3/2, while there were also characteristic modulations, such as the major to the mediant minor, or the major to the flattened submediant, which were constantly used by Sullivan's hero, Schubert. The lyrical appeal of "The sun whose rays" in *The Mikado* is dictated by its irregular phrase-lengths, and by the unexpected modulations that underpin the melody. The "Three little maids" trio in the same opera contains some switchback modulations, too, while each soloist sings in contrasting keys in the quartet "A regular royal Queen" *(The Gondoliers)* to exhilarating effect.

Sullivan's other musical traits included a tendency to overwork some harmonic tricks: in common with all Victorian composers, he over-uses the diminished seventh at dramatic moments. He very seldom couched a whole song or chorus in a minor key, though there are exceptions, including *Ruddigore*'s "When the night wind howls", Katisha's "O Fool", and *Iolanthe*'s almost Verdian "Go away Madam".

In his melodies Sullivan also occasionally used an idiom which the 19th century regarded as true folk song, as in "Prithee pretty

Sargent and Reed captured again during The Yeomen of the Guard recording. One of Sargent's gifts was his ability to give his singers time to breathe in even the most demanding songs and ensembles (above).

maiden" in *Patience,* with its Irish folk-melody plagal cadences, and "I have a song to sing O" in *The Yeomen of the Guard,* are both examples of this; in the first, the setting mirrors Gilbert's inspirational use of folk language, while the second is an instance of a "Green Grow the Rushes O" folksong form of cumulative line-building. The *Ruddigore* duet "I know a youth" and Dick Dauntless' "darned Mounseer" song in the same opera are based on folk or sea-shanty idioms. Another easily recognisable style is that of the English ballad, Sullivan's versions being as gentle and immediately appealing as those of Arne, Dibdin, Storace, or Boyce. Indeed, the resemblance is such that many people, hearing an example by these almost forgotten composers, remark on their similarity to Sullivan.

One of the most typically English choral forms was the glee, and Sullivan frequently uses it in his solo quartets, quintets and, in particular, his "madrigals". The last are more contrapuntal in texture than a true glee, and are liberally sprinkled with fa-la-las, as in "When the buds are blossoming" at the end of Act I of *Ruddigore:* the best-known examples are "Strange adventure", and "Brightly dawns our wedding day". His contrapuntal skill is even more in evidence when combining two melodies in the Maidens' and Dragoons' "Now is not this ridiculous" in *Patience,* in Major-General Stanley's daughters' chatter about the weather while Frederic and Mable, hero and heroine of *The Pirates of Penzance,* become acquainted in "Did ever maiden wake", or in the splendidly bitonal meeting of three tunes in "I heard one day a gentleman say" in *The Mikado.*

SERIOUSNESS AND PARODY

Usually Sullivan's music was aptly suited to the words, but occasionally, he sets a song more seriously than Gilbert intended, as in Lady Jane's "Silvered is the raven hair" in *Patience.* He also absorbed the style of many other composers into his natural musical language. The most popular light opera composers in London had been Wallace, Balfe and Offenbach. Sullivan, however, was less influenced by them in style than by Rossini in the patter songs and the opening chorus of *The Gondoliers,* by Schubert in his use of modulation, and above all by Mendelssohn in the seamless suavity of his melodic line and the deftness of his orchestration. At times his "ensembles of perplexity" as "In contemplative fashion" in *The Gondoliers,* where each character breaks off to express his or her feelings have a Mozartian brilliance. Even Wagner, with whom he had a love/hate relationship, is present in *Iolanthe* – Iolanthe's scene with the Lord Chancellor has been compared with Wotan's Farewell in *Die Walküre* and the funeral march in *The Yeomen of the Guard* to Siegfried's in *Gotterdämmerung!*

Many critics have held that Sullivan's true genius lay in parody, especially of serious operatic composers. The styles of Donizetti and early Verdi, Handel at his most bombastic ("This helmet I suppose" in *Princess Ida*, and in much of *Trial by Jury*), and what Shaw called the "juicy-solemn" church music of Gounod (the "Hail Poetry" chorus in *The Pirates of Penzance)* are all examples of this gift at its most pointed. The virtuosity of coloratura sopranos is gently mocked in Mabel's "Poor wandering one", grand opera recitative in Captain Corcoran's elaborately banal exchanges with Buttercup in *HMS Pinafore*, as well as in Lady Jane's soliliquy (*Patience*, Act II) and in much of *Princess Ida*. "A nice dilemma" has been aptly compared to D'un pensiero in Bellini's *La Sonnambula*, while the opera buffa types of conspirators' chorus are the target in "With cat-like tread" *(Pirates of Penzance)*, and the General's complaint, "but you don't go!" when the imminent departure of the police is constantly announced.

THE ORCHESTRATION OF THE OPERAS

Sullivan's orchestration is particularly felicitous, though often the original scoring is not used, due to the D'Oyly Carte company's retention of the full scores. Though the vocal and instrumental parts were always available on hire to societies wishing to perform the operas, conductors had to work from a cued vocal score only. Indeed, Isadore Godfrey, the Musical Director of the D'Oyly Carte for 43 years, said that he never knew what awaited him in the usual ad hoc orchestra in each venue, and he had to adapt accordingly. It has been noted elsewhere that Sir Malcolm Sargent was accused of adding orchestral "gags" of his own because the instrumental details, especially woodwind interjections, were not in the vocal scores; however, what Sargent did was totally authentic, since he had been allowed to consult the carefully-guarded full versions.

Sullivan's normal scoring was for a small band of strings, two flutes, one oboe, two clarinets, one bassoon, two horns, two cornets, two trombones and percussion. In *The Gondoliers, The Yeomen of the Guard, Utopia Limited* and *The Grand Duke*, this was augmented by an extra bassoon and trombone; Gilbert's reference to Nanki-Poo having disguised himself as a "second trombone" *(The Mikado)* is probably a gentle gibe at Sullivan's perpetual plea for more brass. The woodwind writing is always idiomatic, as in the fairy music in *Iolanthe*, Mad Margaret's attendant obbligatto flute *(Ruddigore)*, the splendidly imaginative accompaniment to the second verse of "When the night wind howls" and the hilarious pair of clarinets in the chalumeau register in "I once was a very abandoned person". There are also the occasionally manic bassoon gurgles in appropriate places, as in Don Alhambra's Act I solo in *The Gondoliers* and the "Three little maids" trio in *The Mikado*.

Sullivan tended to divide flutes and clarinets, so that each played an octave apart. His use of horns was somewhat limited, but the

brass-band tone of the cornets as the original scoring specified produce a much more satisfactory blend than the trumpets that are usually substituted for them today. All in all, Isadore Godfrey was correct, when he commented that "the orchestration is so open that the slightest blemish comes through".

Recurrent Techniques

There were recurrent kinds of numbers in the operas. The patter song was a constant ingredient, and Sullivan set it taking care that the words should be clearly heard. For this reason there is usually a skeleton instrumental support, with the added feature of hilariously repeated chords in a "till ready" style at the start of each song. Occasionally, Sullivan drifts over the thin line dividing economy from banality in his other accompaniments, but often the instru-

Kenneth Sandford leads the male chorus in an ensemble from Trial by Jury during the 1974 recording. This short one-act curtain raiser contains many of the ingredients that were to make the subsequent operas so successful; these included Sullivan's ability to parody the style of other composers, notably Handel and Bellini (above).

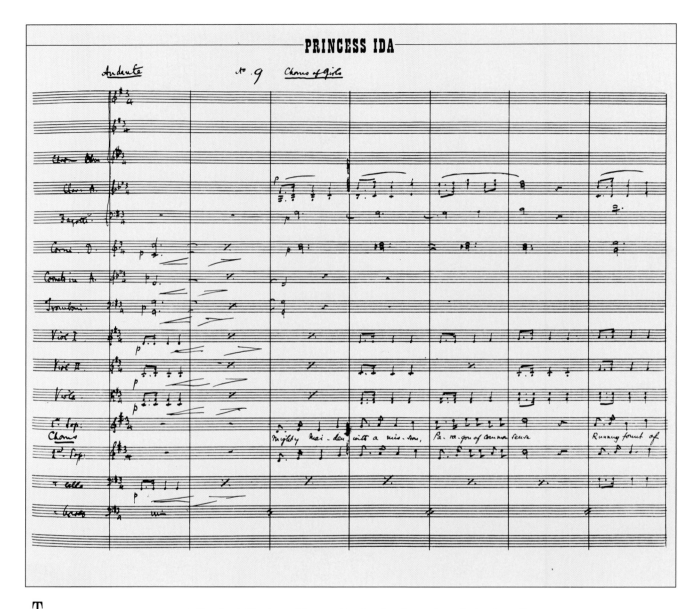

mentation is delicate, with a particular fondness for pizzicato cellos, or violin obbligati above the vocal line, as in the "train of little ladies" in *The Mikado*. He made particularly effective use of tonic pedal as in "I have a Song to Sing O" *(The Yeomen of the Guard)*.

Gilbert ensured in the libretti that the chorus were never static, but Sullivan seized every chance to augment the overall effect, with his use of tarantaras and fa-la-las down to the frequent reiteration of the last words of lines, or corroboratory "Yes! Yes!"s. In the early operas, many chorus settings were unison, but later they were usually harmonised. Often the soprano lead would float over the top of finale choruses to great effect. Shaw maintained that the chorus writing had too high a tessitura, resulting in tenors with "goat-bleat", baritones with "a shattering vibrato" who "could not to save their lives produce a note of any definite pitch", and sopranos who had "the tone of a locomotive whistle without its steadiness".

THE LAST-MINUTE COMPOSER

In contrast to Gilbert's steady and organized approach to the libretti. Sullivan left so much to the hectic last minute that whole sections of the music were often given to the cast the day before the opening night. He apparently mapped out the rhythms suggested by the lyrics, often disregarding the metre and going by the natural accentuation; he often wrote alternative rhythms, and different time signatures. He would then put the music aside, and a few days later would think of an appropriate melody, which he jotted down on the MSS paper pad that he always carried on his person. Eventually, he would harmonise and orchestrate it. Sir Malcolm Sargent remarked that Sullivan took great pains "to avoid hard labour ... He keeps referring one back to previous orchestrations in the score, and one has to be expert to see what is meant". Overtures were frequently left to others, notably Hamilton Clarke or Cellier, to compose, copy or complete. These are often, as in the case of *The Mikado*, a mere bandstand pot-pourri. Those Sullivan did compose are quite different: the *Iolanthe* overture opens with a vague initial tonality – perhaps Sullivan was thinking of a watery version of Haydn's representation of Chaos in *The Creation* – and it has a counter-melody to "O Foolish Fay", which is not in the actual opera. The overtures to *The Yeomen of the Guard, Princess Ida*, the symphonic prelude to *HMS Pinafore*, and the overture to *Patience* were all Sullivan's work.

The contemporary press reaction to Sullivan's music often seems inexplicable today. His obituary said his name was "synonymous throughout Europe with English music" and he was constantly chided for straying from serious composition. When he was knighted in 1883, the *Musical Review* reminded him of his "positive obligation ... to return to the sphere from which he has too long descended". Even Grove felt he should "rally his gifts to a serious opera on some subject of abiding human or natural interest". As early as 1877, *The World* commented sourly: "It was hoped that he would soar with Mendelssohn, whereas he is, it seems, content to sink with Offenbach". Perhaps the caustic Shaw summed it up: "Sir Arthur's school is an exploded one. Neatly and cleverly as he exploits it, he cannot get a progression or a melody out of it that is not the worse for wear." Yet in the end we cannot but agree with that master of musical economy, Debussy, who admired Sullivan in "the clearness of writing, the absence of frou-frou, the almost business-like subjection of means to an end".

Both Sullivan and Gilbert, whatever their differences in methods of work or personality were master craftsmen, with a magnificent sense of the ridiculous. It is our good fortune that their misguided conviction that their real artistic contribution lay in their other characterless works for stage or concert-hall did not prevent their joint creation of the Savoy operas.

The finale of Act II of Princess Ida in the 1954 production designed by James Wade had a determinedly Tennysonian feel (top). Wade, Bridget D'Oyly Carte and stage director Robert Gibson discuss the set model (above.)

CHAPTER FOUR

DECLINE

AND

REBIRTH

U NTIL *PRINCESS IDA*, the relationship between the partners had apparently been an idyllic one. Gilbert was the first to disturb the surface calm by an attack on D'Oyly Carte; he maintained that Carte had too much control over the daily running of the theatre. Carte's reply was characteristically logical and reasonable: "I cannot see how you and Sullivan are part managers of the theatre any more than I am part-author or part-composer of the music."

Gilbert riposted with what was to be a frequent complaint, saying that Carte had risen on the shoulders of the operas. He was not mollified by the reply that Carte was "simply the tradesman who sells your creations of art," and tried to involve Sullivan, in a letter which maintained that the business could easily be ruined by foolish policies. Sullivan reported this to Carte who reminded Gilbert that if there was a mistake, he, Carte, stood the "whole risk of pecuniary loss".

Meanwhile Sullivan was becoming impatient with the type of libretti Gilbert was presenting, and resolved to set no more unless the nature of the plots was radically altered. Though all was temporarily resolved by the inspirational production of *The Mikado* libretto, the basic differences of opinion between composer and librettist were to be a heavy and restless undercurrent beneath the calm surface of their happiest collaborations – of which *The Mikado* was certainly one. Rehearsals throughout the following operas were often acrimonious, partly because of the failing health of both men, for Gilbert was becoming a prey to increasingly frequent attacks of gout, while Sullivan's kidney condition was now almost constantly painful. In addition the two men had to cope with the novel experience of a hostile audience on the first night of *Ruddigore*, and the fact that *The Yeomen of the Guard*, despite their mutual hopes, was not an unqualified success.

In January 1889 a more serious quarrel erupted, again over the relationship and balance between words and music, in which the correspondence was surprisingly choleric from Sullivan as well as Gilbert. Sullivan now demanded that they should work as "master and master" and maintained that he felt a "cipher" in the theatre. However, the natural good-will of both men asserted itself, aided by Carte as mediator, and the result was a reconciliation in May 1889. This time it was *The Gondoliers* that temporarily sealed their reunion – but it was an uneasy peace.

IVANHOE AND THE CARPET QUARREL

Carte had unwittingly reinforced Sullivan's disinclination to write works in which he felt the music was subservient to the words by embarking on a grandiose project to establish a permanent home for English grand opera, for which he built his new Royal English Opera House in Shafesbury Avenue. The obvious choice for the

The screen version of the famous carpet quarrel, which orginated in Gilbert's refusal to contribute to the cost of a new front-of-house carpet for the Savoy. In the Launder-Gillat production "Mr. Gilbert and Mr. Sullivan", Sullivan (Maurice Evans) and Helen D'Oyly Carte (Eileen Herlie) vainly attempt to pacify Gilbert (Robert Morley) and Carte (Peter Finch) (above).

opening work was a serious opera by England's premier composer, who had, after all, been asked by Queen Victoria herself to embark on such a project. Gilbert, with feet more firmly on the ground and scenting problems ahead, felt the scheme was premature, as indeed it proved to be. But somehow Sullivan managed to work both on *The Gondoliers* and progress with *Ivanhoe* at the same time; the latter eventually reached the stage on 31 January 1891. Sullivan himself felt it was "the most important work I have yet written, not only from its magnitude, but also from the strength of the musical work I have put into it". Unfortunately posterity has not agreed with him; even contemporary musicians, like Parry, felt that it was "flat, characterless and inadequate".

Carte moreover had made a serious miscalculation – he imagined that the work would have a long enough run, like the Savoy operas, to allow time for an English follow-up of equal merit to be found. Though *Ivanhoe* ran for 155 performances (by modern standards a startlingly successful number), there was nothing of any stature to put in its place, so Carte had to follow it shamefacedly with a French light opera – Messenger's *La Basoche* – a genre he despised and wished to replace. The theatre was sold to the impresario Sir Augustus Harris, and it dwindled into a music hall.

Even while *Ivanhoe* was being prepared, however, things at the Savoy were moving from bad to worse. The final straw proved to be a pointless quarrel that was followed with avidity both by press and public. Carte's innocent outlay of £500 (later proved to be a mistake and only £140) for new carpets for the front-of-house of the theatre, made according to the agreement of 1883 which gave him full responsibility for such matters, brought Gilbert's subterranean resentments into the open. The latter wrote to Sullivan on 22 April 1890, describing an angry confrontation with Carte, in which he maintained that Carte had insulted him, and (again) did not appreciate that his rise had been due to Gilbert and Sullivan. Sullivan sanely pointed out that most of the production expenses were ordered by Gilbert and nobody had objected to them. He hoped that they could seen meet calmly, but that he agreed with Carte. Gilbert then demanded a new agreement, which Sullivan refused. "The time for putting an end to our collaboration has at last arrived," trumpeted Gilbert and, with true oratorial rhetoric, he mourned that "our united work will be heard in public no more". Sullivan, weary and ill, denied Gilbert's allegation that he had been treated with "contemptuous indifference".

The angry counter-accusations flew thick and fast, until Helen D'Oyly Carte wrote a frank, honest and diplomatic letter to Gilbert, reminding him of the true facts of his initial angry encounter with her husband. The wounded bull was not pacified, and busily conscripted recruits to his cause from the company and the press. He issued a writ against Carte for his share in the profits of the previous quarter in July 1890, but Carte was instructed by his lawyer not to pay, while the embattled Sullivan refused Gilbert's request to join him in asking for a receiver to be appointed to handle the box-office takings for *The Gondoliers*. In the end the unfortunate Sullivan had to give evidence against Gilbert in the resultant legal action on 3 September 1890. After the hearing, Carte paid Gilbert £1000, but, though no receiver was appointed, the partnership lay in ruins. The press sympathised with Sullivan: "The eminent and genial composer of *The Gondoliers* found himself in a warm place just because he happened to be seated near a fire".

A PIPE OF PEACE

However, Gilbert's own natural warmth asserted itself, and he wrote a conciliatory letter to Helen, with a copy to Sullivan, three days after the hearing. All four met, and Gilbert climbed down unconditionally, having gained nothing but the destruction of the existing agreement. He could not resist firing a Parthian shot, arguing that they should all re-examine the expenses since the beginning of the partnership. Indeed, resentment obviously persisted –

for Sullivan reserved two *Ivanhoe* tickets for Gilbert, who brusquely declined them. He repented, for later he asked Tom Chappell to mediate and Sullivan agreed to "meet and shake hands ... we can dispel the clouds hanging over us by sending up a counter-irritant in the form of a cloud of smoke". The outcome of the meeting in October 1891, was the relegation of the carpet quarrel to history, but the old creative urge had gone, and for three years there was no new opera.

THE LAST OPERAS

Meanwhile both men tried working with other collaborators: Sullivan had written the reasonably successful *Haddon Hall* with Sydney Grundy, which was much admired by Shaw, in 1892: he praised the D'Oyly Carte company for its "unmistakeable genius for manage-ment ... at once munificent and economical getting their full pound of beauty out of every yard of costly stuff on the stage". Gilbert had turned to Alfred Cellier for *The Mountebanks*, also with modest success, in which he finally managed to use his beloved lozenge plot, so often scorned by Sullivan. Meanwhile the Savoy theatre was prospering with light opera by both Cellier brothers, and the new star Edward German, who was to complete Sullivan's unfinished opera *The Emerald Isle* after the latter's death.

From this point onwards, Carte seemed to have lost his ability to control his ageing warhorses. They, in turn, had lost their trust in their mutual inspiration, and the result was the verbally brilliant, but only patchily theatrical *Utopia Limited,* which was too clever for its genre in both words and music. The final attempt at collabor-ation was the arid and unsettable *The Grand Duke,* where logical absurdity had become unintelligibly complex, or relied on cliché.

SULLIVAN'S LAST YEARS

From 1895 Sullivan spent much of his time in England at Walton-on-Thames. There was one sentimental interlude abroad the fol-lowing year, when he proposed to a young Englishwoman, Violet Beddington, asking her to cheer his last few years of life in return for being left everything he possessed. She refused him.

Sullivan was still writing operas for the Savoy. In 1898 came *The Beauty Stone,* with a couple of unlikely librettists in Arthur Pinero and J. Comyns Carr, followed by *The Rose of Persia* the next year. Sullivan's increasing frailty (he was only 53) had now forced him to sit while conducting.

By 1898, Sullivan was so ill that he was unable to finish a major composition in time for the Leeds Festival, though he did manage to conduct *The Golden Legend* there; he wrote that "The chorus cheered me so tremendously that I suddenly broke down, and ran off (sic) the orchestra crying like a child". His ill-health forced him to resign the Leeds conductorship. The end came in 1900. Sullivan was working very slowly on his new opera, *The Emerald Isle,* when in October, he caught cold while visiting his mother's grave. His condition deteriorated, and by November 21, he could only whisper. His beloved nephew Herbert notified Sullivan's doctor, who promised to visit the ailing composer the next morning, but at 6am the household were awakened by Sullivan's bell. He called out "My heart! My heart!" and died in Herbert's arms, attended by his servant Clotilde. Poor Fanny Ronalds had to wait for a cab and arrived too late. He was buried in St Paul's at Queen Victoria's wish, despite his request to be with his family in Brompton cemetery. He left an estate of £54, 527.

Meanwhile Carte's health had been failing for the past three years. He managed to drag himself from his sickbed to watch Sullivan's funeral cortege pass by, but died on 3 April 1901 of a digestive complaint and eventual heart-failure. He left the princely sum of £240,817.

The Last Survivor

Gilbert lived on for a further ten years. His creative flame was steadier and less intense than that of Carte and Sullivan, and he was more robust, in spite of being the eldest of the three. His last years were spent happily at Grim's Dyke, surrounded by a private zoo, with antelopes roaming the grounds and pet lemurs sitting on his shoulder while dressing for dinner, hosting lavish children's parties. Emotional, erotic but probably unconsummated relationships with pretty girls were a feature of this time. His protégé, Nancy Mackintosh, for whom the part of Zara in *Utopia Limited* had been disproportionately inflated, became his adopted daughter, and eventual heiress. However, she was clearly equally loved by Kitten, who was apparently unperturbed by Gilbert's roving eye.

Revered and feted, Gilbert received a belated knighthood on 15 July 1907. His death on 29 May 1911 was cruelly premature. He had created an artificial lake in his extensive garden and had invited two of his young lady friends to bathe there. One became frightened when she swam out of her depth, and called for help. The other, a Miss Winifred Emery, recalled later what happened. Gilbert "swam out to her very quickly and I heard him say; 'Put your hands on my shoulders and don't struggle'. This she did but almost immediately she called out that he had sunk under her hand and had not come up. We both called to him but got no answer ... it seemed a long time before they recovered the body". Gilbert had always said he wanted to die on a summer's day in the garden, so such an end, though untimely, would probably have been what he wished. His estate was valued for probate at £111,971 – more than Sullivan's, but much less than Carte's. More importantly, the Carte family had control of Gilbert's copyright, which was to last until 1961.

*J*essie Bond, the original
Mad Margaret in
Ruddigore, photographed
at the time of the first
performance and
Linda-Anne Hutchinson's
1960s version (right).
Ruddigore's revival in the
1920s was one of Rupert's
first steps in rebuilding
the repertory.

THE D'OYLY CARTE TRADITION

After Carte's death, the company was most efficiently managed by
Helen D'Oyly Carte and there were many revivals, notably the rep-
ertory season of 1906–7, when the Lord Chamberlain banned
London performances of *The Mikado* during the state visit of
Japan's Crown Prince Fushimi. Helen characteristically kept the
work in repertory for the provincial tour and, in fact, a Japanese
reporter of the time apparently enjoyed it, rather than taking offence.
From 1909 onwards, when Helen handed over the lease of the
Savoy to C. H. Workman, the company was mainly occupied in
provincial tours and did not return to London for a decade. Rupert
D'Oyly Carte, Helen's stepson took over the management on Helen's
death in 1913, but the outbreak of war the following year put an end
to any plans for the immediate future.

POST- WAR REVIVAL

1919–20 saw the results of Rupert D'Oyly-Carte's wartime planning,
with new sets and costumes designed by W. Bridges-Adams and
Percy Anderson for *Iolanthe* and then *The Gondoliers*. Rupert
himself proved to be an inspired manager. In comparison with his

R*upert D'Oyly Carte, who took over the management of the company after the First World War, proved to be as great an administrative genius as Richard.*

B*ridget D'Oyly Carte succeeded Rupert in control of company affairs. It was her bequest of £1,000,000 that served as the foundation for the re-launch of the New D'Oyly Carte in 1988 (above).*

father, he was introverted and disliked public showing-off; he refused to allow the traditional last-night speeches, for instance. He had been a Secret Service agent in the war and his sang-froid was legendary. When a bomb fell outside during a Board meeting, blasting the curtains out of the window, there was a short silence from Rupert, an equally small cough, and a "Gentlemen shall we continue?" He was philanthropic and often excused small amateur companies their fees and royalties. He died in 1948 at the age of 72 in his suite in the Savoy leaving nearly £300,000 and the performing rights in the operas to his daughter Bridget.

Rupert's reforms were numerous. He started a training school for his singers, insisting that everyone should start off in the chorus. The leading designer Hugo Rumbold was engaged to give *Patience* a completely new look, according to Rupert's new policy of keeping strictly to the original text, but visually updating the appearance of the operas. In 1921, *Ruddigore* was revived for the first time since 1887, in a production which Kitten pronounced to be better than the original. It had a new overture written for it by Geoffrey Toye, the company's musical director, thus continuing the old tradition of overtures being written by other hands. The Savoy proved too small for an immensely successful season, so the Princes theatre became the company's new home until 1929, when it returned to a Savoy redesigned by Basil Ionides, with rows of seating in different colours inspired by the zinnias in Hyde Park, and an April sky painted on the ceiling. Despite such refurbishment, the press seemed to feel that Gilbert was wearing less well than Sullivan; the *Church Times* complained that "there is a curious suggestion of amateurishness in the hallowed gestures of almost all the characters" – a criticism that has been constant ever since.

THROUGH THE YEARS

Rupert was determined to avoid mere imitation of the original stars, though he continued the tradition of putting acting ability, audibility and rhythmic sense ahead of pure vocal beauty. His generation of performers became household names, becoming characters in their own right. One of the longest lived, Henry Lytton (later Sir Henry), a member of the company from 1884–1934, took over the characters originally created by George Grossmith, having been a member of the touring company since the age of 17: apparently there was a "touch of the inspired amateur" about him, characterized by his stage play with his inseparable monocle. "His public was conquered by a winning geniality which was his mortal self."

This cheerful amateurishness was also a characteristic of the original bass lead Richard Temple, who, according to the 1948 memories of Cyril Lely, the son of Durward Lely (the original Nanki-Poo), never finished making up until the very last moment, yet never missed his cue, glueing on the last whisker of beard as he

An on-stage party, held at the Princes Theatre in April 1922. Henry Lytton, the company's leading star, is in the centre; Gilbert's widow is to the left (above).

A packed audience photographed before curtain rise at the Princes Theatre. The company moved here in the 1920s because the Savoy was too small to hold the audiences flocking to its London seasons (left).

THE D'OYLY CARTE IN NORTH AMERICA

Members of the D'Oyly Carte Opera Company at Niagara Falls in January 1928. This was one of the many successful American tours the company made in the 1920s and 1930s. Interest in and love for Gilbert and Sullivan in the USA dates back to the 19th century; indeed The Pirates of Penzance was premièred in New York as Carte's response to the unscrupulous "pirating" of HMS Pinafore by American impresarios, who sheltered behind the law to avoid paying the partners their royalties (above).

Members of the company pose with film star Norma Shearer (second from right) during the 1929 Hollywood visit. She was the wife of MGM boss Irving Thalberg. To the right of Norma Shearer stands Darell Fancourt, whose playing of the Mikado was said to be definitive. Among his innovations was the introduction of a blood-curdling laugh into "A more humane Mikado" (left).

Another photograph of the same Hollywood visit. Here, Henry Lytton (centre) is seen with some of his fellow stars, including Bertha Lewes (third from left), Leslie Rands (second from right) and Fancourt (right). Lytton is wearing his monocle, which also served as an inseparable prop on stage (left).

Nᴇᴡ Yorkers stand in line outside the box office of the Martin Beck Theatre, New York, in 1934. This was the company's first visit to New York for 30 years (top).

Sᴛars of the company in December 1935, ready to open at the Forrest Theatre on Christmas Day. Martyn Green, who succeeded Lytton in the patter roles, is the second from left (above).

1ₐ938 and the company sails across the Atlantic for yet another US tour. Though war clouds were gathering in Europe, the magic of Gilbert and Sullivan still exercised its timeless appeal. By this time, Martyn Green (seated, centre) was well-established as Lytton's natural successor, joining such company stalwarts as Fancourt and Rands (seated next to Green on the right).

Henry Lytton, pictured with Martyn Green, his successor in the great patter roles, on the day of his last performance in January 1933. For many Savoyards, Lytton's style was inimitable and Green wisely developed his own personal interpretations (above).

entered. In Rupert's era, Temple's parts were assumed by Darrell Fancourt, who became "a Mikado that really does curdle the blood" with a voice "like a steam hammer slowly crushing a ton of Brazil nuts and a fiendish gurgling laugh". Brooks Atkinson of the *New York Times* singled this out as "one of the great creations of our time". He performed the part 3,000 times.

The vivacious creator of the soubrette roles, Jessie Bond, must have been a hard act to follow. Rutland Barrington, the tubby first Pooh-Bah, remembered her in *HMS Pinafore,* when she was playing Hebe: "She struck me at rehearsal as being rather a stodgy, not over-intelligent type of girl, showing few signs of the strong personality and great artistic capabilities that were to make her a firm favourite of the public in a short time." It says much for Gilbert's intuition, that, as with George Grossmith and Rutland Barrington, he knew what he wanted in unpromising material. She clearly had quick wits, as she managed to fob off the Prince of Wales' advances without offence. He had asked to visit her and she answered, "My mother would be very surprised if she saw you walking into our house". In fact she lived many miles from her parents. She was nearly sacked from *The Mikado* for asking for a bigger obi, because she liked waggling her obi-bedecked rear at the audience, a demand of which the strait-laced Gilbert disapproved. He made sarcastic comments on her star status, creating equally important "star" roles in *The Gondoliers* to minimise her solo magnetism. She clearly had something of a reputation, for when she was married in 1897 her Quaker father-in-law audibly prayed for her fidelity.

Marjorie Eyre, who took over Jessie Bond's parts after the First World War, had a strong physical resemblance to her predecessor, being petite and dark-eyed, with an ability to be wistful or dramatic. At first she played the straight soprano roles, but over the years her voice deepened and she was a fine Iolanthe, Phoebe and Tessa. She and Bertha Lewis, of the splendidly determined chin, in the "Dame" roles, who sadly died in a car accident in 1931, Winifred Lawson and Leslie Rands all reappear over the next 20 years until a new generation of players grew up, mostly drawn from the chorus, the touring company and understudy ranks, thus retaining the close-knit family tradition of the company.

Martyn Green, Lytton's successor from 1934 onwards, was in the chorus from 1922 and the latter's understudy from 1926. He came from a musical family, but did not see a Gilbert and Sullivan opera until he reached adulthood. His voice was delightful, even though the parts he played – Sir Joseph Porter, the Lord Chancellor, Bunthorne and so on – did not require a fine sound; he was undoubtedly more purely musical than most of the patter leads, showing an unerring sense of timing, coupled with brilliant dancing ability. His acting had more depth than Lytton's, and his Jack Point in *The Yeomen of the Guard* is reputed to have made the critics weep. According to Brooks Atkinson, he was "one of the great Savoy geniuses", while Beverly Baxter hailed him in 1951 as "a great comic and a sensitive artist".

*D*avid Lloyd George, former premier and leader of the Liberal party, presides over a luncheon held to celebrate Lytton's 46-year career in the Savoy operas (left).

*L*ytton was knighted the same year. This is the menu for a celebratory dinner he hosted for members of the company and "a few personal friends" (above).

*S*tars of the 1920s company let their hair down after a recording session. This was in the days before the microphone, when singers were recorded acoustically, literally being propelled away from and towards the recording horn by the studio engineers according to the volume required (above).

In 1951, Peter Pratt took over the Grossmith roles, in the company of singers like Anne Drummond-Grant, who was conveniently married to Isadore Godfrey, and Leslie Rands. He, in turn, was followed by the incredibly versatile John Reed. All these singers have created their own individual characteristics and their individual personalities prevented their interpretation of the parts from becoming jaded.

DIRECTORS OF MUSIC

The first director of music was Alfred Cellier, followed in 1878 by his brother François, who held the post until 1913; both had been Sullivan's lifelong friends since they were boys together at the Chapel Royal. Walter Hann was a caretaker conductor until after the war, when Harry Norris took over the day-to-day musical directorship with Geoffrey Toye, who conducted the 1939 film of *The Mikado,* as a guest conductor. In August 1926, Isadore Godfrey, one of the greatest of all Gilbert and Sullivan conductors, appeared on the scene, staying with the company until his retirement in 1968; he was awarded an O.B.E. for his musical services. Dr Malcolm Sargent

GILBERT AND SULLIVAN AT WAR

When war came to Britain in 1939, most forms of popular entertainment were suspended, though, when no immediate German attack took place, the theatre quickly returned to normal. It took Dunkirk, the fall of France, the battle of Britain and the Blitz the following year to bring the reality of war home. On 17 November 1940, the D'Oyly Carte in its turn suffered, when its Horsely Street warehouse was bombed and its stored costumes destroyed. However, the company, along with Britain as a whole, could "take it", as premier Winston Churchill proclaimed, and performances soon resumed (right).

An open-air performance of The Gondoliers, given in Brockwell Park, in 1942/3. Marco and Guiseppe Palmieri, the twin gondolier heroes of the title, are introducing themselves in the duet "We're called gondoliere" (left).

Tea, cake and sandwiches for the cast, orchestra and audience during the interval of a performance of The Gondoliers. Isadore Godfrey's wife, in ATS uniform (left), is serving tea (left).

The four Allied leaders – Churchill, Roosevelt, Stalin and Chiang Kai-shek – preside over a D'Oyly Carte concert, given in 1942/3. Isadore Godfrey is seated at the piano, surrounded by the company's principal singers (right).

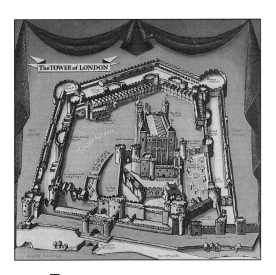

The 1940
commemorative
programme for Rupert
D'Oyly Carte's new
production of The Yeomen
of the Guard featured
Peter Goffin's drop
curtain and its pictorial
map of the Tower of
London. Goffin was in
charge of the whole
production, the aim being
"to re-create a
presentation founded on
the author's original idea,
but more in harmony
with the modern eye".
Goffin's answer was a
basic single-unit set, with
various levels and flexible
acting areas (above).

flashed comet-like across the Savoy sky long before he was knighted, first appearing in 1926 and returning in 1929. He also made some splendid recordings in the late 1920s, in which he adhered as closely as possible to the original, rare full scores. So unfamiliar was the felicitous instrumental detail Sargent revealed that he was accused of inserting orchestral "gags" of his own; in fact, they were Sullivan's, but were often not included, as they were not printed in the vocal scores which were the only material readily available.

Sargent was a guest conductor again in 1950. *The Times* was a little grudging in its praise of him, admitting that he "generally did all that could possibly be done with the unequal vocal forces available". Boyd Neel also occasionally conducted the London season, while Sargent was to share the end of copyright year (1961) with Isadore Godfrey. More recent conductors have been James Walker, Royston Nash and Fraser Goulding; today, Bramwell Tovey, the new musical director, has taken Sargent's work still further, so that Sullivan's scores can be heard as the composer intended.

A CHANGING APPEARANCE

In the original productions, most of the stage and costume ideas came from Gilbert himself, aided by famous names of the time – Hawes Craven, Faustin, Percy Anderson and Henry Emden. One of the most remarkable designers to become involved was Charles Ricketts, whose eye for line and shape was so obvious in his magnificent designs for *The Mikado* in 1926. Ricketts went back to 1720 for his ideas, making much use of stencilled decorations, with cold blues, greens and silvers for the men, and white, bright scarlet and pink for the girls. Katisha's tiger design was particularly beautiful. Ricketts said himself that "an entirely new aspect should be given to *The Mikado* ... the ladies must make-up very white and alter their eyebrows". He objected to the "dreary pink dressing-gown style quite unlike anything Japanese". George Sheringham followed in the 1930s with costumes for the "three Ps" operas – *Pinafore*, *Pirates* and *Patience*.

In 1931 Bridget D'Oyly-Carte had met the designer Peter Goffin at Dartington Hall. She subsequently engaged him for the 1940s productions. His set for *The Yeomen of the Guard* was much criticised as "a Picasso tree and a cement suggestion of the Mersey Tunnel", but Goffin's work fulfilled his brief to produce sets that were "more in harmony with the modern eye"; at the same time, the productions were streamlined and tightened up in speed of dialogue and chorus direction, with use of the set's potential for entrances on different levels. The idea was to use the set to help the production, and not just as a background. Always practical, Goffin designed a "unit set" in 1957 which was usable for all the operas with different additions for each one. He felt strongly that the designer should be part of the production team.

A *Charles Ricketts design illustrated the souvenir programme produced for the 1926 London season. Ricketts was one of the leading theatrical designers of the day, having worked on many straight plays and in grand opera, including a memorable Marriage of Figaro for Sir Thomas Beecham; his engagement was part of Rupert's plan to visually transform the existing productions (above).*

The new costume designs Charles Ricketts produced for the 1926 Mikado were extremely stylish. Ricketts looked back to the 18th century for his colours, the aim being to create the authentic feel of the Japanese prints of that period (left).

A NEW LOOK FOR THE SAVOY OPERAS

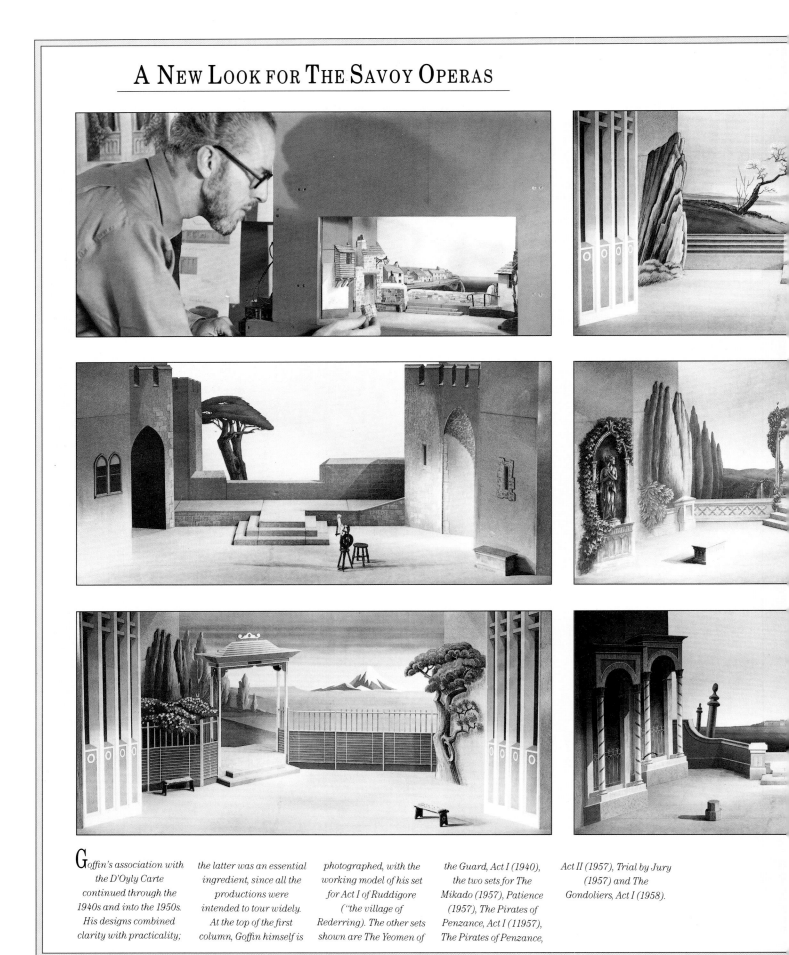

G*offin's association with the D'Oyly Carte continued through the 1940s and into the 1950s. His designs combined clarity with practicality;* the latter was an essential ingredient, since all the productions were intended to tour widely. At the top of the first column, Goffin himself is photographed, with the working model of his set for Act I of Ruddigore ("the village of Rederring). The other sets shown are The Yeomen of the Guard, Act I (1940), the two sets for The Mikado (1957), Patience (1957), The Pirates of Penzance, Act I (11957), The Pirates of Penzance, Act II (1957), Trial by Jury (1957) and The Gondoliers, Act I (1958).

The set for Act I of the Pirates of Penzance looks as though it might have strayed from Wagner's Die Walküre, were it not for the sea in the background and the barrel neatly marked with a skull-and-crossbones stage right (above).

Another 1950s designer, James Wade, created a fantasy world in his Victorian Gothic *Princess Ida*, with "absurd and fantastic costume of a romantic dream or fairy story" and "an amusing travesty of the merely spectacular", according to Bridget D'Oyly Carte. The most startling designer since Wade was Osbert Lancaster whose witty backcloths for *The Sorcerer* in 1971 contained grazing stags in a park in Act I, who appropriately disappeared in Act II's evening set.

THE LAST YEARS OF D'OYLY CARTE

After her father's death in 1948 Bridge D'Oyly Carte assumed full responsibility for the company. She mounted a new version of *Ruddigore* with a new Act II set and costumes by Peter Goffin. Meanwhile the dialogue had come under scrutiny, and A. P. Herbert was engaged to bring it up to date and eliminate possibly offensive words like "nigger". The 1950s marked the start of decline, with tours becoming shorter and less extensive as provincial theatres began to close. Though there were more American tours, the company seemed on the brink of crisis especially with the imminent expiry of the text copyright in 1961 (the music copyright had expired in 1950). Though directors such as Anthony Besch tried to put new life into *The Gondoliers*, introducing bits of stage business

*J*ames Wade's set design for the 1954 revival of Princess Ida – here Act II is shown – was firmly Pre-Raphaelite in inspiration (top left).

*O*sbert Lancaster's set for The Sorcerer (1957) was as wittily mid-Victorian as his costume design for John Wellington Wells.

*L*uciana Arringhi's costume design for the spaghetti-eating Guiseppe of Anthony Besch's 1968 Gondoliers; (above) Arringhi poses with more of her sketches for the production.

Tʜᴇ D'Oyly Carte's
respect for Gilbert's words
was not always total: the
celebrated humourist A. P.
Herbert (seated) was
commissioned to revise
the texts to remove
offensive words, such as
"nigger" (top left).

Cᴇʟᴇʙʀᴀᴛɪᴏɴꜱ in
Manchester in March
1960; Bridget D'Oyly
Carte, assisted by a
heavily made-up Gilbert
and Sullivan, cuts The
Mikado's 75th birthday
cake (above).

Bʀɪᴅɢᴇᴛ D'Oyly Carte was
the doyenne of the
company until her death
(top right).

involving plates of spaghetti accompanying the words "Life is one
complicated tangle", this was only surface gilding.

The flickering flame rekindled itself for the emotional and
evocative Savoy centenary season in 1975, but the axe finally fell in
1982. The company had found it impossible to continue without
public subsidy, but, eventually, there proved to be no money forthcoming, the argument being that the company and its productions
were so old-fashioned as to be unworthy of support. Despite a
"Save the D'Oyly Carte" campaign, the final curtain fell on 27
February 1982.

OUTSIDE THE TRADITION

The critics of the company had had their arguments strengthened
by the success of non-D'Oyly Carte productions. As far back as
1927 there had been the celebrated jazz version of *The Mikado* in
Berlin, with Nanki-Poo portrayed as the son of an American million-
aire, Katisha riding in a car and Yum-Yum bathing more or less
naked. An all-negro jazz version was staged in 1938, sponsored by
the US government to help out-of-work singers and musicians – it

was set on a coral island in the Pacific and was followed by a "hot" Mikado in New York the following year. The unlikely adaptations continued in a jive version of *HMS Pinafore* in 1945 in New York, culminating in the "cool" Mikado of 1962 with Frankie Howerd as Ko-Ko, which left Gilbert intact, but "up-dated" the music. The most successful "pop" version was undoubtedly Joseph Papp's "rock" version of *The Pirates of Penzance*.

More conventional productions also showed the operas in a new light. Sir Tyrone Guthrie directed an eminently theatrical version of *The Pirates of Penzance* at his Stratford, Ontario, Festival in 1961 and the following year the Sadlers Wells Opera staged *Iolanthe* – the first British production following the expiration of the copyright. This had a pantomime transformation scene from Fairyland to Arcady in true extravaganza tradition and, the following year, the company also produced a successful *Mikado*. A magnificently atmospheric *Yeomen of the Guard* was staged *in situ* by Anthony Besch as part of the City of London Festival, with the real Tower of London as backcloth. In recent productions, *Iolanthe* has remained a favourite, as in Scottish National Opera's production, with a Glaswegian Fleta and Rikki Fulton, a well-known Scottish comic, as the Lord Chancellor. The ultimate came when the English National Opera launched Jonathan Miller's 1920s *Mikado* on the world with Eric Idle, then Bill Oddie, as Ko-Ko. Dudley Moore played Ko-Ko when the production was restaged in California.

REBIRTH OF THE TRADITION

In 1982 all the D'Oyly Carte personnel were made redundant, though a small management office was reinstated to maintain the music library, keep the Friends of D'Oyly Carte informed, and to look after

The D'Oyly Carte Company prided itself on its family traditions, a policy the new company also upholds. Here, Bridget D'Oyly Carte and a team of helpers prepare the advance programme mailing for the 1961 Savoy season (top).

Bridget D'Oyly Carte opens "The Gilbert & Sullivan" theme public house in 1962 (middle).

High spirits on tour; members of the HMS Pinafore cast pose on their way to Copenhagen in October 1971 (left).

ROYAL OCCASIONS AND COMMAND PERFORMANCES

Queen Elizabeth II followed in the footsteps of her great-great grandmother when she visited The Gondoliers in 1971, though Queen Victoria had commanded the company's presence at Windsor. Here, the Queen congratulates the cast (above).

The Duke of Edinburgh meets his Spanish counterpart – John Reed as the Duke of Plaza Toro – during the interval of The Gondoliers during the centenary Savoy season in 1975 (left).

The younger royals are also Gilbert and Sullivan fans. Here, Prince Andrew (now the Duke of York) is pictured at the 1975 revival of The Gondoliers (top left).

Frederick Lloyd, Bridget D'Oyly Carte and the Queen examine a presentation set of toast racks at the Royal Command performance of HMS Pinafore in June 1987 (above).

A congratulatory well-done from the Duke of Gloucester to the fairy chorus in Iolanthe after the 1977 first night (left).

FIGHTING TO SAVE THE COMPANY

The threat of closure led to a nation-wide campaign to save the company. Members of the company fund-raising in the piazza in Covent Garden during what was to prove the last season in 1981 (top left and middle right).

Even the eloquence of the House of Lords in the persons of Earls Mountararat and Tolloller failed to move the Arts Council to provide funds – even when supported by a monster petition (top right).

Sir Joseph Porter meets Peter Moore, London's town crier, as part of the fund-raising appeal (middle left), while former Labour premier Harold Wilson lends a hand by launching a prize draw, organized by the Friends of D'Oyly Carte, in December 1981 (bottom).

the warehouse containing all the costumes and scenery. Much of Bridget's property went to the Theatre Museum in London after her death in 1985, while the costumes were sold in January 1984 at a Christie's auction. Meanwhile amateur companies were still using the D'Oyly Carte orchestral parts.

The tradition refused to die, however. Using the income from a million-pound bequest from Bridget D'Oyly Carte, the New D'Oyly Carte Opera Company was reformed under the General Manager-ship of Richard Condon. A sponsor was found in British Midland Airlines, a fine new young music director was appointed in Bram-well Tovey, and casts selected from 1,000 applicants, with help from John Barker of Covent Garden and Victor Morris of English National Opera. In 1988 *Iolanthe* and *The Yeomen of the Guard* were the two operas chosen for the company's debut, with sets and costumes designed by Nadine Baylis and Peter Walker and Christopher Renshaw as the respective directors. The tradition of London sea-sons, and extensive tours – including Broadway in 1990 – is now being relaunched, aided by the donation of £50,000 by the Friends of D'Oyly Carte.

The company in happier mood. Pirate King, Frederic, conductors Fraser Goulding and Sir Charles Mackerras (second from right) celebrate the centenary of The Pirates of Penzance with the stalwart veteran Frederic Lloyd in 1979 (above).

THE SAVOY SURVIVAL

The Savoy operas justify the over-worked description of Phoenix-like. They have survived two world wars and severe financial crises, but seem to retain a place of their own in the British theatrical tradition. One of the reasons for this is their clear links with amateur music-making, both at adult and school levels. Many Gilbert and Sullivan aficionados made their first acquaintance with the Savoy operas at school, where the words, so carefully learnt, are never forgotten. Nor is the phenomenon unique to Britain. In the USA, the works of Gilbert and Sullivan are held in even greater affection – indeed, one of the biggest collections of Savoy memora-bilia in the world is held by the Pierpoint Morgan Library, New York. The operas seem to become part of a kind of Jungian collective unconsciousness of the theatre-going public, wherever they are performed.

They also seem vital enough to stand radical transformation and re-creation, as the success of jazz and rock versions has shown. So what is the secret of their appeal? It cannot lie in the topicality of the satire, as many references need a glossary for full modern understanding. Yet the words of the patter-songs can be effectively updated in the style of Gilbert for contemporary relevance. In common with all durable works of art, their longevity lies in their universal appeal whatever the setting and interpretation.

The characters seem practically interchangeable apart from surface differences, so therefore the strength of the books cannot proceed from portrayal of individual characters. They have the appeal of archetypal pantomime stereotypes – a world in which

Harold Wilson makes the curtain speech at the centenary double bill of Trial by Jury and The Sorcerer at the Savoy in March 1975. The Sorcerer cast is in the background; the sets are by Osbert Lancaster. Even Wilson's eloquence, however, could not persuade the Arts Council to give the company a subsidy and eventually closure became inevitable (above).

Gilbert was trained – on which is superimposed a dizzying verbal inventiveness, and a broad, detached and dehumanised view of purely human frailty. In this lies the secret of their popularity and universality. Gilbert does not hold a mirror up to the shortcomings of particular individuals – he leaves that to the great dramatists – but his detached mockery of general human traits is in many ways less disturbing and therefore more palatable than the uncomfortably personal confrontations of, say, a Shaw or an Ibsen.

One of the sorest points in any new production of a Gilbert and Sullivan opera is whether the tradition of performance, evolved by the close-knit family ideals of the D'Oyly Carte company itself, should be maintained. There are three strands to this tradition – an over-refined style of acting and singing; the retention of complete gravitas and apparent belief in the action, however topsy-turvy, without "ham" or send-up; and the use of traditional stage "business". There is affected coyness of singing and enunciation from the performers in the recordings of the late 1920s, which has no charm, however faded, for today's audience, who merely find it risible and dated: the retention of this style could well mean the death of the operas. But the simply and clean performance of what Gilbert actually wrote is a different matter. The easy solution of a send-up needs to be avoided, for Gilbert knew so well that the wit and punch of his lines would be lost if not interpreted literally and allowed to speak for themselves.

Retention of traditional "business" is perfectly defensible, as long as it is not too rigid. There are those who feel that it is not true to the tradition if the exact number and nature of encores are not followed as laid down by long repetition, and that it is vitally important that Ko-Ko's big toe should remain double-jointed. Perhaps they forget that Gilbert hated "business" that was not in the original or approved by him later (he enjoyed Grossmith's backward squatting run with the teapot as John Wellington Wells): he insisted on fining cast members who introduced gags of their own. Yet it is such gags, like Darryll Fancourt's laugh in *The Mikado*, which was not used until 1924, that are incorrectly regarded as traditional. As with all works of the past, if the image of the character is true, then it is effective.

There are often differences in traditional musical tempi, from Sullivan's original markings, though he was often known to alter speeds in rehearsal. It is here, therefore, that a long tradition of performance may be valuable: but in the end verbal audibility must be the guide. The point has often been made that music can bear more repetition than words, yet the aficionados can repeat Gilbert's libretti by heart with as much pleasure as they can sing Sullivan's melodies. Music does not "date" if it is good, so the reason for the appeal of the operas must undoubtedly lie partly in the memorability of Sullivan's music, despite its formulae and clichés.

Most of all, the partnership was unique in its chemistry. Hoffmansthal aided and inspired Richard Strauss, Boito partnered Verdi, Da Ponte, Mozart and Eric Crozier, Britten, but nobody has ever claimed that these librettists were of equal stature to their composers. When we hum a composer's melody, we do not necessarily recall the text: Sullivan's tunes are inseparable from the words, and in this lies the perennial appeal of the operas.

Their relevance today is decided by whether their satire is transposable to modern institutions, recurring human dilemmas or follies. The prime example is *Patience*, which has been successfully adapted to mock hippy culture. Adaptations of this opera will always find a target where there are followers of cults who have assumed the trappings, rather than the spirit, of their cause and in the process have also mislaid their sense of humour.

Ernest Newman, the great Wagner critic, sums up the problems of too rigid an adherence to tradition: "Just as a character is capable of as many interpretations as there are great actors to interpret it, so a play as a whole is capable of as many productions as there are producers of genius. The trouble with a tradition is that in time it becomes not a guide but a fetter."

Today the reborn D'Oyly Carte is showing every sign of throwing off these fetters, while retaining the true spirit of the conception of the operas.

Company patter stalwart John Reed, costumed as Ko-Ko, one of his most celebrated creations, poses with his golden disc, presented to him by Decca to celebrate his 25th anniversary in 1977 (top).

Reed's Bunthorne for the last night of Patience in 1968 reflected the then prevailing spirit of "flower power" rather than that of Swinburne and Oscar Wilde (above).

BACKSTAGE BEHIND THE FOOTLIGHTS

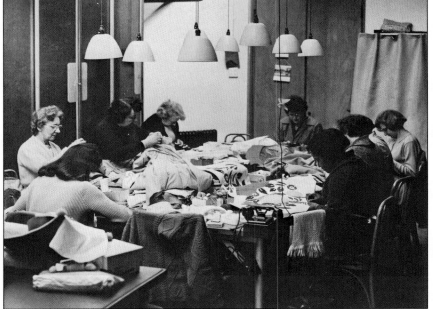

Every opera company has unseen stars behind the scenes, whose role is just as vital as that of the stage principles Ruby Buckingham, wardrobe mistress of the D'Oyly Carte company for many years, was a typical example (top left).

Keeping the company's costumes spick and span was a backstage essential, especially given the demands of touring. Here, the wardrobe seamstresses are hard at work, keeping the costumes for The Mikado in trim (top right).

A member of the wardrobe team presses a blouse for a member of the chorus. The costume hanging on the dummy at the back belongs to one of Sir Joseph Porter's tribe of 'sisters, cousins and aunts' in HMS Pinafore (above left).

Harry Haste was the company's master carpenter and assistant stage manager from 1926. Here, he is translating a design sketch into practical reality (above right).

*G*ilbert had a mania for authentic detail: while preparing HMS Pinafore, he took Sullivan to Portsmouth, so that both men could study HMS Victory. Here, the scenery painters are adding the finishing touches to the painted rigging.

D'Oyly Carte pioneered the use of electricity in the theatre and the lighting plot was consequently always important. Peter Riley, shown here at the lighting console, rose from the ranks to become the company's deputy general manager (top right).

*T*he traditional call of 'overture and beginners please' signals the start of another performance and the excitement mounts backstage as well as in front-of-house. Here, the contadine make up before a performance of The Gondoliers (above left).

*T*he chorus of dragoons in Patience find various ways of passing the time before they make their rousing entrance as the "Soldiers of the Queen" in Patience (above right).

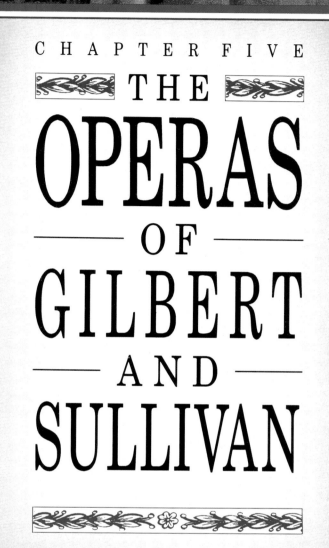

CHAPTER FIVE

THE
OPERAS
OF
GILBERT
AND
SULLIVAN

THESPIS

OR THE GODS GROWN OLD
GAIETY THEATRE (26 DECEMBER 1871) 64 PERFORMANCES

DRAMATIS PERSONAE

— GODS —

JUPITER, *Aged Deity*	MR JOHN MACLEAN
APOLLO, *Aged Deity*	MR F SULLIVAN
MARS, *Aged Deity*	MR WOOD
DIANA, *Aged Deity*	MRS H LEIGH
MERCURY	MISS E FARREN

— THESPIANS —

THESPIS	MR J L TOOLE
SILLIMON	MR J G TAYLOR
TIMIDON	MR MARSHALL
TIPSEION	MR ROBERT SOUTAR
PREPOSTEROS	MR H PAYNE
STUPIDAS	MR F PAYNE
SPARKEION	MDLLE CLARY
NICEMIS	MISS CONSTANCE LOSEBY
PRETTEIA	MISS BEREND
DAPHNE	MISS ANNE TREMAINE
CYMON	MISS L WILSON

ACT I – Ruined Temple on the Summit of Olympus

ACT II – The same Scene, with the Ruins Restored

GILBERT AND SULLIVAN's first meeting in 1869 at German Reed's Gallery had not been productive and Reed had not been successful in his suggestion that the two men should collaborate. It was left to John Hollingshead, the manager of the Gaiety Theatre, a "licensed dealer in legs, short skirts, French adaptation, Shakespeare ..." and a believer in cleaning up the theatre, to achieve the coup of the first Gilbert and Sullivan collaboration.

The theme of gods changing places with humans was more of an opéra-bouffe subject than a burlesque one – Offenbach constantly plundered classical mythology, giving his gods comically human characteristics, and the results were very popular in London. There is little contemporary reference, unlike later Gilbert, except to the Duke of Sutherland who, as a lover of railway trains, inspired the first of Gilbert's patter songs, with a trundling metre and a cast apparently imitating a steam engine. There is one comment on social inequality; this anticipated one of Gilbert's later preoccupations in Mercury's "celestial drudge" song:

"Though noodles are baroned and earled

There's nothing for clever obscurity"

The role of Thespis contains some rueful detail on the tribulations of a stage-manager, which, no doubt, were drawn from Gilbert's personal experience.

Gilbert was already trying to reform the role of the chorus by making its members part of the action – until then they merely stood until they were required to sing. The cast were Hollingshead's regulars, with the comedian J. L. Toole as Thespis plus Fred Sullivan, Arthur's brother, as Apollo. There were pantomime elements as well; Nellie Farren, as Mercury, took the main principal boy role; there were some fireworks with Jupiter's thunderbolts, and the public were familiar with the traditional clown and harlequin roles, Preposteros and Stupidas.

Thespis, however, was not a success. The opera was under-rehearsed, being put on stage in three weeks. "Few actors in the cast could sing, and of those who pretended to, hardly any could be said to compass more than six notes," said the depressed Gilbert. The audience in the gallery and pit missed all the jokes, as they had never heard of the Greek gods. At Christmas, such an audience expected straight pantomime acrobatics and tunes they knew, not entirely new music. Finally, the piece overran for an hour. It was solidly and firmly booed.

The music has been lost. Sullivan asked Hollingshead for the parts, which were never returned, but he was later to utilize the first chorus in *The Pirates of Penzance*. One ballad ("Little Maid of Arcadee") was published separately and still exists. Apparently the music was witty and imaginative, but Sullivan said he felt "rather restricted as a composer in having to write vocal music for people without voices".

There was one appreciative member of the audience, however. Richard D'Oyly Carte felt the opera had been unfairly treated, and given a better cast and production, would have stood a very good chance of being a success. When Gilbert appeared in his office four years later, with a libretto under his arm, Carte was delighted to remind him of the composer of *Thespis*.

SYNOPSIS

A chorus of stars comes wearily off the night shift to a somewhat derelict Mount Olympus, followed by a down-at-heel Diana and an ageing Apollo, who are both finding their duties extremely burdensome. An equally tired Mercury, loaded with parcels of age-alleviating remedies for the gods, bewails his role as "the celestial drudge" for nobody else does any work. The ancient Jupiter agrees with him, grumbling that mortal sacrifices have dwindled down to "preserved Australian beef". They are alarmed by Mars announcing the advent of a party of humans, and hide in a ruined temple.

Sparkeion and Nicemis, members of a touring company of actors, appear, quarrelling because Nicemis rejects Sparkeion's advances as they are "not quite married", though the company is to celebrate their wedding with a feast on the mountain. They bicker over Nicemis' jealousy of Sparkeion's past liaison with Daphne. The company appears with its manager, Thespis, at its head, singing "Climbing over rocky mountain". Over their picnic, Thespis has to deal with a drunken actor. A potential argument between the jealous lovers is forestalled by Thespis' tale of the Chairman of Directors of the "North South East West Diddlesex Junction", in which the company give a lively imitation of a train. Jupiter, Mars and Apollo appear dramatically in their godlike guise, but Thespis, who is in full flight on his role as manager, dismisses them patronisingly like out-of-work actors, who are not impressive in their parts, saying they need to be more up-to-date if they are again to command human respect. They arrange, in a quartet with Diana, to swop places with the mortals for a year; Mercury will remain as a consultant if necessary, and Sparkeion will become Apollo, Nicemis, Diana and Daphne, Calliope.

Act II sees the Thespians happily playing at gods in a splendidly restored version of the Act I set. But they are "improving" on the age-old function of the gods – the sun is shining at night, for example, because the deputy Diana needs Apollo for company. Sparkeion, who has not been at all faithful to Nicemis, sings of the ability of human hearts to heal in "Little Maid of Arcadee". Mercury confirms in a song that "Olympus is in a terrible muddle", for Thespis, as Jove, has remained unaware of the year-old complaints that are piling up.

Meanwhile Daphne has found a book that says Apollo (Sparkeion) was married several times and that Calliope was one of his

AN EVENING OF EXCERPTS *from the D'Oyly Carte repertoire:*
Cox & Box 1866 ✧ Thespis 1871 ✧ Trial by Jury 1875 ✧ The Sorcerer
1877 ✧ HMS Pinafore 1878 ✧ The Pirates of Penzance 1880 ✧ Patience
1881 ✧ Iolanthe 1882 ✧ Princess Ida 1884 ✧ The Mikado 1885 ✧
Ruddigore 1887 ✧ The Yeomen of the Guard 1888 ✧ The Gondoliers
1889 ✧ Utopia Limited 1893 ✧ The Grand Duke 1896 ✧ ✧ ✧ ✧
*and including a Concert Overture based on Savoy Opera themes composed
by Paul Seeley*

PRINCIPAL ARTISTES ~ Kenneth Sandford ✧ John Ayldon ✧ James
Conroy-Ward ✧ Lorraine Daniels ✧ Clive Harré ✧ Patricia Leonard ✧
Peter Lyon ✧ Meston Reid ✧ Geoffrey Shovelton ✧ Vivian Tierney ✧ ✧ ✧
GENTLEMEN OF THE CHORUS ~ Clive Birch ✧ Neil Braithwaite ✧
Michael Buchan ✧ Barry Clark ✧ Philip Creasy ✧ Alistair Donkin ✧
Robert Gibbs ✧ Bruce Graham ✧ Michael Hamlett ✧ Peter James-
Robinson ✧ Michael Lessiter ✧ Thomas Marandola ✧ Guy Matthews
Sean Osborne ✧ Alan Rice ✧ Thomas Scholey ✧ ✧ ✧
LADIES OF THE CHORUS ~ Pamela Baxter ✧ Susan Cochrane ✧
Linda Darnell ✧ Riona Faram ✧ Christine George ✧ Alexandra
Hann ✧ Suzanne Houlden ✧ Beti Lloyd-Jones ✧ Margaret Lynn-
Williams ✧ Roberta Morrell ✧ Jill Pert ✧ Jane Stanford ✧ Ann-
Louise Straker ✧ Caroline Tatlow ✧ Hélène Witcombe ✧ ✧ ✧

The programme for 27 February 1982 featured excerpts from all the operas in the D'Oyly Carte repertoire, though it was stretching things to include Thespis, which had remained unperformed – bar two numbers – since its London première, the score having been lost (above)

wives. A quartet quarrelling over the women's rival claims ("You're Diana, I'm Apollo") is settled by Thespis allotting Sparkeion to Nicemis when he is a god and to Daphne when he is mortal. The gods now reappear in disguise and check with Mercury that Thespis has not heeded his advice at all during the year. They settle down to hear the enormous bundle of petitions from Earth, which Thespis perfunctorily dismisses with amusingly makeshift excuses and solutions. The gods are so angry that they unmask, and banish the Thespians from Mount Olympus with the terrible curse that "You shall all be eminent tragedians Whom no one ever goes to see". The opera ends with a reprise of the chorus of the Diddlesex Junction song.

TRIAL BY JURY

A NEW COMIC OPERA

ROYALTY THEATRE (25 MARCH 1875) 300 PERFORMANCES

DRAMATIS PERSONAE

THE LEARNED JUDGE .... MR F SULLIVAN

COUNSEL FOR THE PLAINTIFF .... MR HOLLINGSWORTH

THE DEFENDANT .... MR W FISHER

FOREMAN OF THE JURY .... MR KELLEHER

USHER .... MR PEPPER

and

THE PLAINTIFF .... MISS NELLY BROMLEY

BRIDESMAIDS

GENTLEMEN OF THE JURY

SCENE – A Court of Justice

BETWEEN the première of the ill-fated *Thespis* and the beginning of 1875, Gilbert had written many straight plays, including *Pygmalion and Galatea, The Wicked World* and *Charity*. Sullivan had composed a *Te Deum, The Light of the World* and the incidental music to *The Merry Wives of Windsor*. Richard D'Oyly Carte, meanwhile, was managing a series of light operas at the Royalty Theatre, and, by chance, was looking for a suitable curtain-raiser for his production of Offenbach's operetta *La Périchole*.

Gilbert happened to call on Carte for some advice. He had recently been expanding one of his Bab Ballads, written for *Fun*, into a short libretto and wanted Carl Rosa (founder of the famous opera company of the same name) to compose the music for it. Unfortunately, Rosa's wife, Mme Parepa-Rosa, who had given Gilbert his first writing experience, had just died, so Carte, who had seen *Thespis* and felt it had deserved a better reception, suggested Gilbert might contact Sullivan instead. Gilbert duly called, rather defensively, script in hand, on Sullivan at his new flat in Queen's Mansions.

Sullivan wrote in his diary: "He read it through to me in a perturbed sort of way with a gradual crescendo of indignation in the manner of a man considerably disappointed in what he had written. As soon as he came to the last word, he closed up the manuscript violently ... apparently unconscious that I was screaming with laughter the whole time". Sullivan was so enchanted that he set to work that day, finishing the composition in three weeks. A unique triumvirate, whose sum was greater than its parts, had been created as a result of a coincidence and a death.

The lessons of *Thespis* had been learnt. Two whole months were allowed for rehearsal, free from the Gaiety pantomime traditions that the *Thespis* cast had endured, and Christmas, too, was well past. The audience was changing and was better educated and therefore could appreciate wit rather than slapstick. Gilbert himself was quickly achieving better standards of production, sets, costumes and acting in his other work. Fred Sullivan, Arthur's brother, was also quite outstanding as the Judge, but sadly died after 128 performances. As a result Sullivan did not compose for many months, and then produced the ballad *The Lost Chord* in memory of his brother.

The plot was essentially the fruit of Gilbert's disastrous legal years; it must have been satisfying for him both to parody the system in which he had failed to forge a career so dismally, and to attack savagely the methods by which a judge could succeed. The devious path to success taken by the judge was later paralleled in the careers of Sir Joseph and the Major General. The piece is also a very bitter attack on Victorian dual morality. The jury do not object to the Defendant's inconstancy, merely regarding it indulgently as the typical behaviour of a young rake; nor do they protest at his

"Monster, monster, dread our fury, here's the Judge and we're the Jury". The Defendant and jurymen clash, the Judge and Usher look on, while the jilted Angelina sits demurely with her counsel and bridesmaids (stage left). The Judge's eventual solution is to tell the assembled company to "Put your briefs upon the shelf. I will marry her myself!" (left).

description of the "marriage tether". This has a far more biting cynicism than the affectionately mild mockery of later works.

There is an almost surreal gravity in characterisation, setting and action. In the foreword to his farce *Engaged,* Gilbert suggests that comedy should be "played with the most perfect earnestness and gravity throughout ... Directly the actors show that they are conscious of the absurdity of their utterances, the piece begins to drag". This avoidance of exaggeration contributed greatly to the success of Gilbert's revolutionary and disciplinarian production techniques in the operas.

This is the only opera without spoken dialogue. Even so the music matches the verbal parody with various targets of its own. The gaiety of contemporary operas by Lecocq and Flotow would be more easily recognized by the audience of 1875 than today, when they are as forgotten as last year's hit musical. But the Handelian pomposity of the Judge's entry, and the Italian floridness of Bellini, Donizetti and even early Verdi, are instantly identifiable, as are the Offenbach-style galop rhythms. There were original musical traits, too. The first chorus is often on one note enabling the words to be clearly heard – so much for Gilbert's later assertions that his words were subservient to the music! The inspired swings of mood and metre in the text were not only set sympathetically by Sullivan, but enhanced by adding another dimension of musical commentary on the action.

The public knew that this was a new and superior type of entertainment. "It seems as though poems and music had proceeded from one and the same brain," said one critic, while another stated, "laughter more frequent and more hearty was never heard in any theatre". *The Times* stoutly claimed that England had produced a rival to Offenbach, which was Carte's dearest dream.

SYNOPSIS

In a Court of Justice, the chorus of barristers, court officials, spectators and jury await the start of a breach of promise case. They are harangued by the Usher on impartiality, while clearly being directed to find for the Plaintiff. The Defendant ("When first my old love I knew") is partially successful in gaining their sympathy, but he is interrupted by the Judge's appearance to general acclamation ("All hail great Judge"). He responds by telling the court the somewhat shady ruses he employed to assist him in his rise to eminence ("When I, good friends, was called to the bar"). After the jury are sworn in, the Plaintiff, Angelina, with her chorus of bridesmaids, is called into court ("Comes the broken flower"); she is clearly recovered enough to be susceptible to new attentions. She collects all her bridesmaids' wreaths, which she places on the heads of the jury, while the Judge sends amorous notes to the first bridesmaid, then switches his attentions, with the jury's approval, to Angelina

"*When first my old, old love I knew*". The rascally defendent thinks it perfectly reasonable that he should eventually find his original sweetheart "*a bore intense*" and then become "*another's love-sick boy*" (top left)

"*Comes the plaintive flower*". Angelina, Trial by Jury's heroine, is quick to flirt with the judge, but indignantly objects to the proposal to make the Defendant tipsy to see if he will live up to his claim to "*beat her and kick her*" when "*in liquor*" (Middle left).

herself. Counsel for the Plaintiff pleads her case ("With a sense of deep emotion"), punctuated by Angelina's sobs on his manly chest, before she falls, by invitation and half-fainting, onto the Judge.

The Defendant, pleading his own case ("Oh gentlemen, listen I pray"), manages to persuade both judge and jury that it is only natural for a young man's affections to stray, and offers, as a solution, to marry both his old and current sweethearts. The Plaintiff's Counsel, however, points out that marrying two wives at once is "Burglaree", and a quartet of Defendant, Plaintiff, Judge and Counsel all agree that "A nice dilemma we have here". The Defendant's protestations that "I smoke like a furnace – I'm always in liquor" are a desperate measure to repel the Plaintiff's rapturous declaration of renewed love. The Judge's suggestion that they make the Defendant tipsy and await the results, is regarded as objectionable by all, so he provides the ultimate solution – he will marry the Plaintiff himself – a pronouncement received with general agreement that "of such as she" he is "a good Judge too".

"*With bias free of every kind, this trial must be tried.*" The Usher's instructions to the jury are contradictory to say the least (bottom left).

"*With a sense of deep emotion*" of the responsibilities of his task, Angelina's counsel embarks on his opening speech to the jury. Both the court and his "*interesting client*" are deeply moved by his appeal (above).

THE SORCERER

AN ENTIRELY ORIGINAL MODERN COMIC OPERA
OPERA COMIQUE (2 NOVEMBER 1877) 178 PERFORMANCES

DRAMATIS PERSONAE

SIR MARMADUKE POINTDEXTRE, *An Elderly Baronet* .... MR TEMPLE

ALEXIS, *of the Grenadier Guards – His Son* .... MR GEORGE BENTHAM

DR DALY, *Vicar of Ploverleigh* .... MR CLIFTON

JOHN WELLINGTON WELLS, *of J. W. Wells & Co., Family Sorcerers* .... MR GEORGE GROSSMITH

LADY SANGAZURE, *A Lady of Ancient Lineage* .... MRS HOWARD PAUL

ALINE, *Her Daughter – betrothed to Alexis* .... MISS ALICE MAY

MRS PARTLET, *A Pew-Opener* .... MISS EVERARD

CONSTANCE, *Her Daughter* .... MISS GIULIA WARWICK

CHORUS OF PEASANTRY

ACT I – Grounds of Sir Marmaduke's Mansion

ACT II – Market-Place of Ploverleigh

(Half-an-hour is supposed to elapse between Acts I and II)

TIME – The Present Day

B ETWEEN *Trial by Jury* and 1877, Sullivan had seen the
extraordinary success of his ballad *The Lost Chord,* had
become as famous a conductor as composer and had been
awarded a doctorate of music by Cambridge University. Gilbert was
busy with revivals of his own plays, notably his favourite *Broken
Hearts,* and had also written a short story called *An Elixir of Love,*
based on the general theme of Donizetti's opera *L'Elisir d'Amore,*
which he had translated in 1866 as a burlesque.

By 1876, Carte was so encouraged by the success of *Trial by
Jury* that he was realizing what had seemed an impossible dream –
"the starting of English opera in a theatre devoted to that alone".
He formed the Comedy Opera Company with a syndicate consisting
of Tom Chappell, George Metzler (both music publishers), Augustus Collard the piano maker, and the picturesquely named Edward
"Watercart" Bailey, so dubbed because he had the virtual monopoly
of the cleaning of the London streets. Carte's role at this stage was
not managing director, but secretary and adviser. Each of the syndicate put up £5,000 and they took a lease on the Opéra Comique.
In June, Carte, Gilbert and Sullivan drew up an agreement for the
writing of a new two-act opera.

The theatrical idea of the love-potion, which was to be a permanent bone of contention between composer and librettist in the

*"It is done!" John
Wellington Wells creates
his love philtre, while
Alexis and Aline look on.
A contemporary critic
commented: "The scene is
a rich burlesque on some
operatic incantations, the
whole piece being an
amusing caricature,
which is made the vehicle
of much pungent satire
and playful wit... and of
the very clever music
which Mr. Arthur
Sullivan has written to it"
(above).*

The "Captious Critic" of The Illustrated Sporting and Dramatic News reviewed the double-bill of The Sorcerer and Trial by Jury in 1884, the first time the two operas were performed together at the Savoy.

shape of Gilbert's so-called "magic lozenge" plot, was a heavily worked one, but Gilbert extracted his own magic potion from it in the witty text and the creation of one character who was to be one of the funniest in all the Savoy operas – John Wellington Wells, the lovable "dealer in magic and spells" with a line in Petticoat Lane sales-patter. Gilbert was unwittingly establishing types that were to reappear in the operas again and again. Though partly his creations, it was the actors he engaged to play them who added, on Gilbert's admission, their own personalities to the roles, and this was never more the case than in the choice of George Grossmith to play Wells.

He was a respectable young pianist/entertainer, who had caught Sullivan's eye while playing the Judge in *Trial by Jury* in an amateur performance. His audition was somewhat unconventional: "Sing this" said Sullivan, playing a D, and Grossmith did so. "Beautiful," said Sullivan. "Can you do that?" he asked, having sung "My name is John Wellington Wells" to the bewildered Grossmith, who said he could. He was promptly hired, but he was worried about his acceptance – "If I fail I don't believe that the YMCA will ever engage me again!" He need not have worried: one of the most popular Savoy stars and creator of all the "patter" roles, he was the first to incorporate "business" into his part – his unrehearsed backwards run with the teapot, while making steam-train noises, was one of the few *ad lib* gags that Gilbert allowed to remain in the performance.

The trio of Grossmith, an inexperienced young actor called Rutland Barrington, who played Dr Daly, and Richard Temple, who was an opéra-bouffe singer, dominated the stage in the Gilbert and Sullivan operas for the next ten years. It says much for the identical inner vision of both men that they instinctively sensed the potential of what they wanted when confronted by inexperienced players. The general framework of the cast was established at this time – the soprano, mezzo, contralto, tenor, light baritone, baritone and bass covered all exigiencies.

The plot had some pantomime elements. Wells, for instance, was descended from a Demon King, albeit a friendly one, with his explosives and tricks, but Gilbert's wit lay in making him an honestly brash tradesman. Dr Daly is an original and credible human being, and the inarticulate love between Sir Marmaduke Pointdextre and Lady Sangazure, whose name sounds as if she has stepped out of *The Rivals*, is touchingly human. She is the first and most attractive of Gilbert's middle-aged ladies, who became increasingly unlovely and grotesque in the unsuitability of the objects of their affections; at least Lady Sangazure has dignity and her love is reciprocated.

There is a certain amount of topicality in the plot – the original of the Wells family firm is the Beecham family from Lancashire who were making a fortune as a result of their advertising campaign for their patent medicines and "little pills". In addition the evangelical temperance movement was news, though the intoxicating effect of an apparently harmless pot of tea was borrowed from a tea-inspired "knees-up" in Gilbert's 1868 burlesque of *The Bohemian Girl*, or *The Merry Zingara*. His topsy-turvy humour is already evident in the pairing of incongruous couples under the influence of the love-potion in the second act. Incidentally, ecclesiastical opinion of the time felt he had not treated the church, as personified by Dr Daly, with true reverence.

The music is a little dull compared with the libretto, but there are some attractive dances – Dr Daly's little Purcellian minuet in Act I and the decorous duet of the elderly lovers. The music for the incantation scene is a straightforward parody of the Wolf's Glen

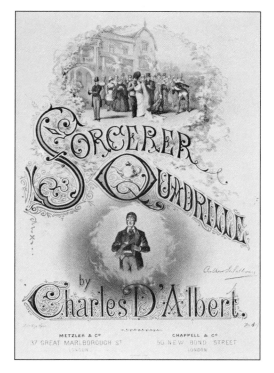

Sullivan's songs were the pop hits of their day, much as Gilbert's sallies became part of everyday conversation. This quadrille was a typical pot-pourri of the time, arranged for the home pianist (top).

Leo Sheffield, the Dr. Daly of the 1919 revival, plays his flageolet (above).

scene in Weber's *Der Freischütz*. Sullivan never completely discarded the prop of parody when writing comic opera.

The reviews were favourable, especially for Barrington and Grossmith, and for Gilbert's painstaking care over production, clarity of diction and avoidance of exaggeration. Above all the lack of smuttiness in the text was noted and approved. Though Sullivan's music was regarded as spontaneously springing from the action, there were already ominous mutterings about the "downward path" that Britain's young white musical hope was treading. It was a path that was to bring him immortality, as well as the money to conduct his high society life-style, but he was to despise it all his life.

SYNOPSIS

The chorus celebrate the betrothal of Alexis and Aline, the scions of the Pointdextre and Sangazure families. Constance confides the secret of her love for the vicar, Dr Daly, to her mother, the pew-opener, Mrs Partlet ("When he is here"). Though Dr Daly is middle-aged, he still remembers the time "When Love and I were well-acquainted", but he was "a pale young curate then"; it is clear from the kindly detachment of his conversation with her mother, that Constance's love is not returned.

Alexis' verbose paen of love for Aline contrasts with the excessive reticence of his father, Sir Marmaduke, which forbids any declaration of mutual love between him and Lady Sangazure. Aline and her friends appear and rejoice "With heart and with voice" at Aline's "happy young heart". The open emotion of the young lovers is again contrasted with the taut formality of their parents' decorous love duet ("Welcome joy, adieu to sadness").

Left alone with Aline, Alexis sings of his longing for a universal love that will break down class barriers ("Love feeds on many kinds of food, I know"). He feels that only a love philtre could achieve such a result, and he has asked an old family firm of sorcerers to concoct it for him. The Sorcerer, manager of the firm J. W. Wells and Co., has a strong line of Petticoat Lane patter in his introductory sales talk ("My name is John Wellington Wells"). The magic potion is brewed in a large and homely teapot on a darkened stage lit by flashes and dramatic interjections from a chorus of spirits. The stage lightens again for the celebrations ("Now to the banquet we press"), during which Dr Daly brews a separate small pot of tea.

"My name is John Wellington Wells". The Sorcerer introduces himself to Alexis and Aline as "a dealer in magic and spells", reeling off a catalogue of his magical powers and the goods he has on offer (below).

"With heart and voice". The chorus in Act I rejoices in Aline's good fortune in becoming betrothed to Alexis; she describes her feelings in her opening aria (above).

The rest drink deeply from the large teapot ("Eat, drink and be gay"), but soon begin to feel the effects of the potion and the curtain falls as they all lie apparently asleep.

Act II, set in the village market-place, opens with a dance of ill-assorted couples in terms of both age and social station, who nevertheless assert "Happy are we in our loving frivolity". Constance, now helplessly in love with "a very deaf old man" (the local notary), is the only unhappy member of the ensuing ensemble ("Oh joy! oh joy!"). Alexis now unwisely insists that Aline, too, must drink the potion ("Thou hast the power"), but in the meantime a puzzled Dr Daly enters, his bewilderment increasing when confronted with Sir Marmaduke and Mrs Partlet demanding instant marriage ("I rejoice that it's decided"). Mr Wells, meanwhile, is horrified at the effects his philtre has produced, especially when Lady Sangazure herself falls in love with him ("O agony, rage, despair"). Aline, frightened of losing Alexis' love, now swallows the philtre, but meets, not her lover, but a pensive Dr Daly instead ("O my voice is soft and low") with the inevitable result. Even Alexis' embrace ("Alas that lovers thus should meet") fails to shake Aline's infatuation and, amid general confusion, Mr Wells proclaims that the only antidote is death – his or that of Alexis and nobly goes to Hell, swallowed up in red fire like Mozart's Don Giovanni. Immediately the spell is broken and the various couples pair off more suitably, singing of the joys of the feast to come ("Now to the banquet we press").

"Now to the banquet we press"! Dr. Daly, Sir Marmaduke and Lady Sangazure celebrate the betrothal of Alexis and Aline at the start of the Act I finale (top right).

The love philtre begins to take effect, as the chorus and principals start to slump to the ground and fall into a deep sleep (right).

H.M.S. PINAFORE

OR THE LASS THAT LOVED A SAILOR

OPERA COMIQUE (28 MAY 1878) 571 PERFORMANCES

DRAMATIS PERSONAE

THE RT HON SIR JOSEPH PORTER, KCB *First Lord of the Admiralty* .... MR GEO GROSSMITH, JUN

CAPT. CORCORAN, *Commanding H.M.S. Pinafore* .... MR RUTLAND BARRINGTON

RALPH RACKSTRAW, *Able Seaman* .... MR POWER

DICK DEADEYE, *Able Seaman* .... MR R TEMPLE

BILL BOBSTAY, *Boatswain's Mate* .... MR CLIFTON

BOB BECKET, *Carpenter's Mate* .... MR DYMOTT

TOM TUCKER, *Midshipmite* .... MR FITZALTAMONT

SERGEANT OF MARINES .... MR TALBOT

JOSEPHINE, *The Captain's Daughter* .... MISS E HOWSON

HEBE, *Sir Joseph's First Cousin* .... MISS JESSIE BOND

LITTLE BUTTERCUP, *A Portsmouth Bumboat Woman* .... MISS EVERARD

FIRST LORD'S SISTERS, HIS COUSINS, HIS AUNTS, SAILORS, MARINES, &C.

SCENE – Quarter-deck of *H.M.S. Pinafore,* off Portsmouth

ACT I – Noon

ACT II – Night

THE SORCERER had been running for only five weeks when Gilbert began planning the next opera. Like all good theatrical businessmen, he borrowed freely from his own plots. He reverted to the *Bab Ballads,* using elements from *Captain Reece, Joe Golightly, General John, The Baby's Vengeance, The Martinet, The Bumboat Woman's Story* and *The Sailor Boy to his Lass* in the construction of the new story. Carte immediately approved it, while Sullivan, though "insensible with pain" from kidney stones and impoverished by his gambling in Nice, set to work, shelving a Leeds Festival commission for a new oratorio in order to do so. His hectic creative pattern for the future was fast emerging.

Gilbert's own pattern of meticulous attention to detail was already established, however, and he took Sullivan down to Portsmouth in April 1878 to see *H.M.S. Victory,* noting every detail of the ship, the uniforms of officers and men and the traditional routines of the crew. Now he could write roles with particular performers in mind – for instance, Sir Joseph Porter was tailor-made for George Grossmith. With his eye for new talent, Gilbert invited Jessie Bond, destined to be one of the greatest of Savoy stars, to play Hebe, Sir Joseph's first cousin.

The opera's main target was class distinction, as expressed through Gilbert's reliance on reversed social stations in a typically topsy-turvy plot. However, it is also typical that the established order, although shaken, is upheld. Breaking through the class barrier is obviously regarded as unsuitable, for the old order triumphs with the discovery that Ralph is actually an aristocrat by birth. Sir Joseph preaches equality to Corcoran, because he knows nobody can be regarded as equal to himself ("Never mind the why and wherefore").

The origins of Sir Joseph's character are equally interesting. The real First Lord of the Admiralty of the day was W. H. Smith, who, like Sir Joseph, had never been to sea, was known to be of humble origin and owed his rise to the founding of the chain of newspaper and stationery shops that still bear his name. Gilbert apparently believed that by making him a radical First Lord, rather than a Conservative one, nobody would connect role and model. However, Benjamin Disraeli, the Prime Minister, was quick to dub the unfortunate First Lord "Pinafore" Smith.

A notable feature of the effect of the text was the public adoption of its catchphrases. The crew's challenging "What never?" to Corcoran's boasts, answered by a sheepish "Well, hardly ever", became common parlance. There is even a bizarre anecdote of the future Kaiser Wilhelm II greeting Sullivan, during a visit to Germany, with an offer "to polish up the handle on the big front door".

Gilbert's name still appears before Sullivan's on the first night programme, and though the opera's melodies have proved popular, many are musically less distinguished than in later works. Sullivan's blandness and sentimentality can take the sting out of the verbal satire, as in Ralph's parody of operatic ballads in "A maiden fair to

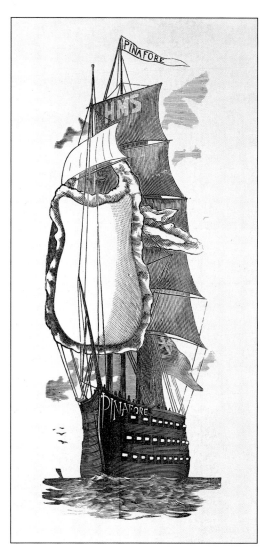

"We sail the ocean blue and our saucy ship's a beauty"! A sight never yet seen on the Gilbert and Sullivan stage – HMS Pinafore herself in full sail (above).

"We're sober men and true and attentive to our duty". Goffin's costume design for a member of HMS Pinafore's crew is the central feature of this D'Oyly Carte hoarding poster. Note the straw hat, which was official Royal Navy wear at the time (above).

see". Buttercup's most famous song ("I'm called Little Buttercup") is somewhat trite, though, in fairness, it is only intended as a glamorized street cry. However, the tongue-in-cheek spirit of patriotism is excellently caught, while the trio "Never mind the why and wherefore" is a classic example of a genre in which Sullivan was to excel. He was also exploring a standard formula at a climax, allowing a floating solo soprano line of his heroine to rise above the chorus.

Rehearsals went well on the whole, though the dress rehearsal continued until a frantic 3.35 am. On one occasion Barrington was asked to rest his considerable bulk in a "pensive manner" on a frail piece of scenery – and broke it. Gilbert's muttered riposte was that he did not say "*ex*pensive". The first night was well received and reviews hailed the opera as the best yet. The *New Era* pointed out that "Mr Gilbert and Mr Sullivan have worked together in the true spirit of collaboration. The former's ... words are really wedded to the music, not sacrificed to it. Mr Sullivan has entered into the spirit of the jest". The chorus' participation in the action was praised (Gilbert always insisted that it should not be static) and Grossmith, Barrington and Helen Everard as Buttercup were dubbed by *The Times* "a trio of genuine humorists".

All boded well, but the box-office was slow – perhaps because it was a long hot summer, and the Opéra-Comique entrance was down an equally long hot tunnel. Also, the audience was not yet accustomed to topsy-turvy humour. The directors of the syndicate pressed Carte to close the opera and it is a measure of his vision and persuasiveness that they agreed to cut their salaries by a third instead. The tide turned when Sullivan conducted a suite from the opera at a Covent Garden concert: it was encored five times and the box office was besieged the next day by a new, fashionable audience. Everybody whistled the tunes and Carte was pestered for permission to perform by amateur companies. "Pinafore mania" had begun.

The Americans were not slow to profit from the reversal in *Pinafore*'s fortunes. The score was copied and performed in Boston on 25 November 1878, followed by numerous productions all over the USA. By the following March the Philadelphia correspondent of *The Times* burbled (with a marked lack of syntactical grace) that "Such a furore as this opera has created I have never known in the history of the American people". Unfortunately, not only were there no US laws to protect the partnership's copyright, but the libretto was also adapted to suit particular circumstances. In Boston, for instance, Ralph was played by a girl, as in the old burlesques from which Gilbert was determined to escape.

Carte decided to show the USA how it should be done, but unfortunately, although well received, the genuine version only ran for a few weeks, since most people had already seen the pirated operas. There was also opposition to the British intrusion from the obvious vested interests. On the company's triumphant arrival in

New York's harbour, surrounded by ships with banners hailing the opera and bands playing the *Pinafore* melodies, a raucous protest was made by one boat hired by a minstrel version. It tried to drown the music with a loud whistle while sporting a "No *Pinafore*" banner.

Carte meanwhile had renewed the sub-lease of the Opéra-Comique and appointed a new manager, Michael Gunn, to whom he gave power of attorney. He then left Britain to sort out the American situation. The directors of the syndicate immediately sacked Gunn and announced that Carte was no longer the manager. A legal battle ensued, with a dramatic climax.

Both the company's lease of the theatre and the agreement with Carte were due to expire on 31 July 1879. During that evening's performance, there was a commotion backstage. A gang of thugs hired by "Watercart" Bailey tried to remove the scenery and the props. They appeared at the prompt entrance and terrified the ladies of the chorus. But the boarders were duly repelled with all the doughtiness of the true British tar by the stage hands and male chorus, while Buttercup firmly went on singing. Cellier, the conductor, finally stopped the performance, and Grossmith asked the

"Oh joy and rapture unforseen, the cloudy sky is all serene". The Act I finale of HMS Pinafore sees Josephine finally admit that she returns Ralph's love. The chorus rejoice, but Dick Deadeye (stage left) plots to expose the lovers' planned elopement to the Pinafore's captain (above).

audience to remain in their seats while the battle raged backstage. The unfortunate stage manager Richard Barker was injured while leading the defenders, but the scenery was saved and the performance continued to loud cheers from the audience. The result of the fracas was the break-up of the Comedy Opera Company and the drawing-up of a partnership agreement between Gilbert, Sullivan and Carte.

There is an amusing corollary. A "Children's Pinafore" opened in December 1879 and was very popular. But it offended Lewis Carroll, who was "sad beyond words" at "sweet innocent girls . . . singing with bright happy looks . . . Damn me, Damn me".

SYNOPSIS

The crew of *HMS Pinafore* sing while scrubbing the decks ("We sail the ocean blue"). They stop to greet the bumboat woman, Little Buttercup, as she peddles her wares ("I'm called Little Buttercup"). She hints at a dark secret that only she knows. After the appearance of the villainous crew member Dick Deadeye, the young sailor Ralph Rackstraw sings of his love for the Captain's daughter ("A maiden fair to see"). Captain Corcoran enters ("I am the Captain of the *Pinafore*"), and is congratulated by his crew on his lack of seasickness and his avoidance of "a big big D" which he "hardly ever" uses. He admits to Buttercup his sadness at his daughter Josephine's lack of enthusiasm at the prospect of marriage to Sir Joseph Porter, First Lord of the Admiralty. Josephine too, is sad ("Sorry her lot"), for, as she tells her father, she loves a humble member of the *Pinafore's* crew.

Preceded by pomp and his female relations, Sir Joseph enters to describe how he rose to his present lofty position ("When I was a lad I served a term"). He asks to meet Ralph as a fine upstanding crew member, but tries, being of a Radical political inclination, to alter the Captain's peremptory manner when giving the crew orders. Ralph is encouraged by all but Dick Deadeye (who has some pertinent comments on equality) to declare his feelings to Josephine. After the glee "A British tar is a soaring soul", Ralph is rejected by Josephine. ("Refrain audicious tar"). He is not comforted by the encouragement of the chorus and Cousin Hebe. Meanwhile Josephine has struggled with her snobbery, and stops Ralph's threatened suicide by admitting her love for him. They plan to elope that night despite Dick Deadeye's gloomy predictions of disaster, which all brush aside.

Act II opens on deck in the moonlight, with a pensive Captain Corcoran confiding his problems to the moon, while Buttercup pines for him in the shadows. He tells her he is aware of her affection for him, but cannot return it because of her lowly social station. She reminds him that "Things are seldom what they seem," but he fails to understand her hints. Sir Joseph testily protests at Josephine's

A later "ruler of the Queen's Navee" – Martyn Green as Sir Joseph, photographed during an American tour of the 1930s.

"For I hold that 'If you please'..." A politically radical First Lord, Sir Joseph is determined to introduce politeness into the giving of naval orders. Here, he is reproving Captain Corcoran for swearing (above).

lack of interest in his suit, but listens unseen as she sings of the difficulty of her choice between riches and poverty ("The hours creep on apace"). Sir Joseph misunderstands her, and, together with her father, reassures her that lowly rank is no bar to marriage ("Never mind the why and wherefore").

Dick Deadeye shatters the Captain's satisfaction with the warning of the imminent elopement. Both hide as the crew, Ralph, Josephine and Buttercup steal stealthily in, then confront them. Ralph stalwartly declares his love and the Boatswain and crew sing of Ralph's pride in being an Englishman. The thwarted Captain swears ("Why, damme it's too bad") to the horror of Sir Joseph who dismisses him ignominiously to his cabin; on learning from Ralph of his love for Josephine, Sir Joseph orders his imprisonment. After Ralph has bade an emotional farewell to Josephine, all is saved by Buttercup's revelation of her guilty secret in "A many years ago," when she "practised baby-farming". Carelessly, she had "mixed up" two babies of low and patrician rank. They were Ralph and the Captain – but it is Ralph who is "upper crust". Sir Joseph's snobbery prevails over his emotions and he hands over Josephine to Ralph with some relief. Cousin Hebe's promise to comfort his declining years is not entirely welcome, but he is resigned to his fate. The final pairing between the Captain and Little Buttercup is neatly arranged and all rejoice in a reprise of "He is an Englishman".

"I am the monarch of the sea". George Grossmith, creator of the role of Sir Joseph Porter KCB in the original 1878 production.

"My pain and my distress". Despite having assured Josephine that "love can level ranks". Sir Joseph is horrified to discover she truly loves "a common seaman" (left).

THE PIRATES OF PENZANCE

OR THE SLAVE OF DUTY

ROYAL BIJOU THEATRE, PAIGNTON (30 DECEMBER 1879),
FIFTH AVENUE THEATRE, NEW YORK (31 DECEMBER 1879),
OPERA COMIQUE (2 APRIL 1880) 363 PERFORMANCES

DRAMATIS PERSONAE

RICHARD, *A Pirate Chief* .... MR BROCOLINI

SAMUEL, *His Lieutenant* .... MR FURNEAUX COOK

FREDERIC, *A Pirate Apprentice* .... MR HUGH TALBOT

MAJOR-GENERAL STANLEY, *of the British Army* .... MR J H RYLEY

EDWARD, *A Sergeant of Police* .... MR F CLIFTON

MABEL, *General Stanley's Youngest Daughter* .... MISS BLANCHE ROOSEVELT

KATE, *General Stanley's Daughter* .... MISS R BRANDRAM

EDITH, *General Stanley's Daughter* .... MISS JESSIE BOND

ISABEL, *General Stanley's Daughter* .... MISS BARLOW

RUTH, *A Piratical "Maid-of-all-Work"* .... MISS ALICE BARNETT

GENERAL STANLEY'S DAUGHTERS, PIRATES, POLICEMEN, &C.

ACT I – A Rocky Seashore on the Coast of Cornwall, England

ACT II – A Ruined Chapel on General Stanley's Estate

THE BIRTH of *The Pirates of Penzance* was even more complex than that of the other operas in the Gilbert and Sullivan canon. When Sullivan took Gilbert's new libretto with him to New York in November 1879, he discovered that he had left his sketches for Act I in London, so there was nothing for it but to start afresh. He managed to rewrite everything from memory, except for the entrance chorus for the Major-General's daughters. Resourcefully, he substituted "Climbing over Rocky Mountain" from *Thespis,* thus preserving one of the only two *Thespis* pieces still extant. He finished Act II by working till 5.30 am over Christmas 1879, so enabling the first copyright performance to take place – in Paignton on the Devon coast of Britain. One of Carte's touring companies, which had been rehearsing *HMS Pinafore* in Torquay, hurried along the coast, topped their *Pinafore* costumes with piratical coloured handkerchiefs and sang (from band parts rushed over from the USA) to a bewildered audience of 50 at a chilly midwinter matinée. All orchestral parts and copies of the libretto were then locked away to avoid unlawful copying. The copyright coup had been organised by Helen Lenoir, helped by Carte's acting manager, George Edwardes. She was so efficient that Carte sent her for her to join him in the USA, where she stayed for six years, organizing company tours.

Meanwhile in New York, the American pirates were being foiled by their British counterparts. All Gilbert would divulge to an avid American press was that, as before, he intended to "treat a thoroughly farcical subject in a thoroughly serious manner". He bor-

*P*olice and pirates proved irresistible comic fare for 19th–century Londoners and New Yorks. Both elements are prominently featured on the front cover of the programme of the first London production in 1880 (above).

"*W*e seek a penalty fifty-fold". Determined to revenge themselves on Major-General Stanley for having deceived them into believing he is an orphan, the pirates march on his country mansion.

"Hush hush, the Major-General comes". Racked by guilt at his disloyalty to his ancestors by falsely telling the pirates he is an orphan, the distraught Major-General prays for forgiveness in the ruins of the family chapel in Act II. Here, Martyn Green is photographed in his Act II costume (above).

"Have you ever known what it is like to be an orphan?" The quick-wits of the "model of a modern Major-General" are put to the test by the Pirate King In Act I (right).

Members of the 1961 cast pictured by the plaque commemorating the first performance of The Pirates of Penzance at Paignton, Devon, in 1879 (right).

rowed the main idea of the plot from his own work *Our Island Home*. This had been written for German Reed's family to perform in 1870, and concerned a long-lost son bound by a pirate oath to kill everyone on the island until he reaches his 21st birthday. Like Frederic, Captain Bang has an over-developed sense of duty. Gilbert had also translated Offenbach's opera *The Brigands,* which had a similar plot.

Naturally enough, Gilbert injected new elements into his basic plot. The lugubrious Cornish policemen who feature prominently are amongst the most touching and funny of Gilbert's creations; even though they do not appear until Act II, their entrance is always eagerly awaited. Again the plot is based on topsy-turvydom; the mistaken apprenticeship of Frederic to a pi*rate* rather than a pi*lot*, the ridiculous logic of his leap year birthday, and the automatic condoning of the pirates' lawlessness when it is discovered that "They are all noblemen gone wrong" are classic Gilbertian ingredients.

The established types of character are also in evidence. Ruth is a particularly cruel example of the middle-aged "inamorata", but Major-General Stanley, in his dithering indecision, is more sympathetic than his prototype, Sir Joseph Porter. The cast were also the company regulars, with Rutland Barrington as the Police Sergeant and Richard Temple as the Pirate King. Sadly, Helen Everard, as Ruth, fractured her skull in one of the final rehearsals, when a piece of scenery fell on her. She eventually died, and Emily Cross took over the part at 24 hours notice.

The contemporary criticism that the opera was "Pinafore on dry land" is a valid one. The hero and heroine are still conventional, but neither tenor role is particularly likeable (Gilbert hated tenors). The Pirates are a land-locked version of the *Pinafore's* crew; the police sergeant is the counterpart of Corcoran's gentle baritone: the sisters and cousins and aunts become the Major-General's daughters, and superficially Sir Joseph Porter merely switches services to become a Major-General.

The obvious satiric focus is on the army and the police force, but there are other contemporary references; Frederic talks of scuttling the Cunard Steam-Ship company which had been reformed in 1878. There is even mention of "that infernal nonsense *Pinafore*". The Major-General's "model" was probably the publicly admired Sir Garnet Wolseley, who had published a military organization manual in 1869 and led the British in the Ashanti wars in 1873. Grossmith was give a similar waxed moustache and told to imitate his manner. Wolseley apparently relished this unexpected publicity.

The music still contains many parodistic elements. The Pirates' determinedly loud "cat-like tread" has counterparts in many contemporary light operas – *Marietta*, Offenbach's *Madame L'Archiduc* and even the *Barber of Seville*. "Poor Wandering one" is a colora-

"*O better far to live and die under the brave black flag I fly!*" The Pirate King decorates the 1941 D'Oyly Carte Manchester programme.

The playbill for the first British performance. Gilbert later changed the sub-title to "The Slave of Duty"

tura aria in the best Italian *bel canto* tradition. The Major-General's ballad "Sighing softly to the river" has one of Sullivan's most attractively murmuring accompaniments. Music so good is all the funnier for being written with Grossmith's rather inadequate vocal equipment in mind. Overall Sullivan considered the music "infinitely superior in every way" to that of *HMS Pinafore*, but, as in the earlier opera, the orchestration is heavily brass-laden. The overture was not finished until the early hours of the day of the first New York performance, with the help of both Alfred Cellier and Frederic Clay, and rehearsed for the first time six hours later.

This time there was no uncertainty over the opera's success: the audience now knew what to expect of Gilbert's humour. As Clement Scott in *Theatre* remarked: "He shows us all that is mean and cruel and crafty and equivocal even in the world's heroes; and he makes us laugh at them because we are convinced such faults are lingering in the breast of the best of us". For its part, *The*

"A *policeman's lot is not a happy one". The bumbling Sergeant and his timorous policemen are among the most inspired of Gilbert's comic creations (top).*

F*rederic, in his Act II uniform, is determined to exterminate his former friends (above).*

A *pensive Pirate King, the leader of a soft-handed band of orphaned "noblemen who have all gone wrong" (right).*

Standard praised the music: "How completely Mr Sullivan enters into the spirit of his companion's words … even the simplest airs are rescued from being commonplace by the piquant and skilful orchestration." Both of these comments, made in 1880, are equally valid today.

SYNOPSIS

On a rocky Cornish shore a group of pirates toast the end of the young pirate Frederic's apprenticeship at his coming-of-age. The reason for Frederic's mixed feelings on reaching this milestone is explained by his beloved ex-nurse Ruth ("When Frederic was a little lad"). When receiving her master's orders for his son's future career, she misheard "pi*lot*" as "pi*rate*". Frederic explains that once free to do so, he is in honour bound to exterminate his pirate friends. But first he enlightens them on the reasons for their lovable lack of success. They are too soft-hearted in avoiding attack on those weaker than themselves – especially orphans, for they, too, are parentless. Ruth wants to leave with Frederic, but as she is the only woman he has seen, he is uneasy over her middle-aged devotion. The Pirate King, despite Frederic's pleas, refuses to give up his way of life ("O better far to live and die").

Left alone with him, Ruth almost convinces Frederic that she is a fine figure of a woman, but in the distance the daughters of Major-General Stanley appear. Frederic angrily dismisses Ruth, for he sees how beautiful they are and realizes she has deceived him. The girls are enjoying their exploration of the seashore ("Climbing over rocky mountain") and prepare to paddle. Frederic surprises them and reassures them that he is a reformed pirate. Mabel, in her

Mabel in "Poor wandering one" (below).

Frederic and Mabel plight their troth in Act I (above).

"**O**h, is there not one maiden breast?" Frederic's plea for understanding is eventually answered by

"With cat-like tread upon our prey we steal!" Ruth, the Pirate King, the reluctant Frederic and Samuel, the Pirate King's lieutenant advance on the Major-General's country house, the chorus of police unseen in the background (above).

"When Frederic was a little lad". Ruth's career as a nursemaid came to an untimely end when, mis-hearing her instructions, she apprenticed him to a pirate, rather than a pilot. In remorse, she enlists in the pirate band (left).

coloratura aria "Poor wandering one" expresses her love and sympathy. She and Frederic retire into a cave to converse, and her sisters ostensibly discuss the weather, while trying eagerly to listen. They are interrupted by the Pirates, who seize them as their brides. Their abduction is prevented by the advent of their father, who is, he assures them, "the very model of a modern Major-General". Obviously, he objects to acquiring pirate sons-in-law and has also heard of the key to the pirates' collective heart. Accordingly, he claims that he, too, is an orphan. All kneel in a suddenly serious moment ("Hail Poetry, thou heaven-born maid") leading to his acceptance as an honorary pirate. Meanwhile Ruth's plea for forgiveness has again been spurned by Frederic and she creeps away amid the general celebration.

Act II is set in a moonlight-bathed ruined chapel. The Major-General's guilty conscience over his duplicity is excused by his daughters and Frederic, who is still determined to exterminate his former friends. He has enlisted the services of the local police who march in with courage-boosting "tarantaras" and are encouraged by all to go forward into reluctant battle with their foe. Frederic, now alone, is accosted by the Pirate King and Ruth in "When first you left our pirate fold". They are helpless with laughter at their discovery of "A most ingenious paradox". The term of Frederic's apprenticeship was determined by birthdays and, since he was born on 29 February, he is only five-and-a-quarter years old, and therefore still in service to the pirates. As the slave of duty and a reborn pirate he is compelled to tell them of the Major-General's lie,

"Yes, forward on the foe"! The Sergeant and supporting chorus overcome their natural timidity and pluck up courage to tackle the pirates. This shot was photographed on Blackpool beach in 1981 (left)

T*he Pirate King, here
shown on D'Oyly Carte
advertising material, is
one of Gilbert and
Sullivan's most instantly
recognizable characters
(above left).*

P*irate King and Samuel
do not seem totally
overjoyed at the prospect
of a return to civilization
and respectability (Act II)
(above right).*

M*abel and her sisters
pose for the camera,
determined to help
redeem the "poor
wandering ones". (right).*

and they rush off to organize vengeance ("Away, away my heart's on fire"), while Frederic is torn between love and duty ("Away, away ere I expire"). He explains his dilemma to Mabel, who begs him to stay ("O leave me not to pine"), but he promises to claim her when he is free ("In 1940, I of age shall be"). The police again march in to be told of Frederic's defection, and the Sergeant bewails the unhappiness of the policeman's lot ("When a felon's not engaged in his employment"). The police tarantaras are reduced to a frightened pianissimo by the appearance of the pirates with their fortissimo "cat-like tread". The defenceless appearance of the conscience-stricken Major-General in a dressing-gown, seeking the source of the noise and singing of Nature's peace ("Sighing softly to the river"), followed by his daughters in white peignoirs does not deter the pirates and they triumph in the ensuing fight. But the effect of the Sergeant's demand on them to yield "in Queen Victoria's name" is instant obedience – "Because with all our faults, we love our Queen". They are saved from punishment by Ruth's timely declaration that "They are all noblemen who have gone wrong", and as such are now suitable sons-in-law for a Major-General!

"In 1940, I of age shall be". Frederic's sense of duty compels him to return to the pirate fold once the paradox of his leap-year birthday has been revealed. However, he and Mabel swear to be true to each other until his final release from his apprentice indentures (left).

"In fact, when I know what is meant..." The Major-General is quick to anticipate the pirates' intentions of carrying off his daughters by force and to devise a counter-plot to deal with the situation (Act I) (above).

PATIENCE

OR BUNTHORNE'S BRIDE

OPERA COMIQUE (23 APRIL 1881) 170 PERFORMANCES
TRANSFERRED TO SAVOY THEATRE (10 OCTOBER 1881) 408 PERFORMANCES

DRAMATIS PERSONAE

COLONEL CALVERLEY, *Officer of Dragoon Guards* .... MR RICHARD TEMPLE

MAJOR MURGATROYD, *Officer of Dragoon Guards* .... MR FRANK THORNTON

LIEUT. THE DUKE OF DUNSTABLE, *Officer of Dragoon Guards* .... MR DURWARD LELY

REGINALD BUNTHORNE, *A Fleshly Poet* .... MR GEORGE GROSSMITH

ARCHIBALD GROSVENOR, *An Idyllic Poet* .... MR RUTLAND BARRINGTON

MR BUNTHORNE'S SOLICITOR .... MR G BOWLEY

CHORUS OF OFFICERS OF DRAGOON GUARDS

THE LADY ANGELA, *Rapturous Maiden* .... MISS JESSIE BOND

THE LADY SAPHIR, *Rapturous Maiden* .... MISS JULIA GWYNNE

THE LADY ELLA, *Rapturous Maiden* .... MISS FORTESCUE

THE LADY JANE, *Rapturous Maiden* .... MISS ALICE BARNETT

and

PATIENCE, *A Dairy Maid* .... MISS LEONORA BRAHAM

CHORUS OF RAPTUROUS MAIDENS

ACT I – Exterior of Castle Bunthorne

ACT II – A Glade

I N HIS next libretto, *Patience,* Gilbert turned his attention to a contemporary target. In 1848 Rossetti, Burne-Jones, Swinburne and Morris had founded the Pre-Raphaelite brotherhood in a "back to Nature" reaction against the ugliness of Victorian industrialization and materialism. The smothering richness of Victorian art, architecture and furnishings was to be supplanted by simple, naturally shaped and preferably handcrafted artefacts, furniture and fabrics. Of course, these aims were laudable and the founders of the brotherhood talented, visionary and serious people. But, as in all strongly characterized movements, the superficial appurtenances, not the spirit, were seized on by the dilettantes and poseurs within artistic society, the result being exaggerated admiration of fascinating decadence (as in the unexpected sensuality of some of Swinburne's poetry), the muted colours of Whistler or the swirling draperies of Burne-Jones paintings. When Walter Pater jumped on the aesthetic band-wagon and urged Oxford undergraduates to burn "with a gem-like flame", the genuinely emotional became trite or pretentious. In 1878 Oscar Wilde came down from Oxford and became the focus of the movement. "Oh would that I could live up to my blue china," he mourned.

Gilbert was not the first to look to the movement as a plot inspiration. In 1880, F. C. Burnand, the librettist of *Cox and Box,* staged *The Colonel,* a parody with an "aesthetic" villain, while George Du Maurier had satirized the movement in *Punch.* Gilbert's twist was to incorporate the idea of a rivalry between two poets, borrowing the notion from his *Bab Ballad, The Rival Curates,* which he had abandoned as a potential libretto in case it met with church disapproval. There are still echoes of the original in *Patience;* the raffle has the atmosphere of a church fête, while Grosvenor is described as "sanctified" and "canonical". In *The Sorcerer,* Dr Daly had described the parish maidens gazing upon him "with rapt adoration" and "forsaking even military men" and the idea is carried forward into *Patience,* where the atmosphere is of the erotic, but unconsummated, emotion of mediaeval romance.

Gilbert, however, was careful not to go too far. In a note appended to the first night programme, it was stated that the new movement had "latterly given play to the outpourings of a clique of professors of ultra-refinement who preach the gospel of morbid langour and sickly sensuousness, which is half real and half affected by the high priests for the purposes of gaining social notoriety. The authors of *Patience* have not desired to cast ridicule on the true aesthetic spirit, but only to attack the unmanly oddities that masquerade in its likeness".

The costumes were influenced by Burne-Jones paintings, and also by the sophisticated illustrations to traditional nursery rhymes in Walter Crane's *The Baby's Opera* (1877). As later for *The Mikado,* all the fabrics were chosen from Libertys. Their "tender bloom like cold gravy" shades were a splendid contrast to the dragoons' pri-

T*he original poster for the opera (top).*

"H*e will have to be contented with a poppy or lily". Frank Thornton, the dashing dragoon Major of Act I, undergoes an aesthetic transformation along with his brother officers in Act II. Thornton created the role of Major Murgatroyd in 1881 (above).*

"Twenty love-sick maidens we". Julia Gwynne created the role of the Lady Saphir in the 1881 first production.

"If you're anxious for to shine in the high aesthetic line". George Grossmith's depiction of Reginald Bunthorne, a "fleshly poet", captivated no less a person than Oscar Wilde.

mary colours. There has been much discussion as to whether or not Bunthorne stands for Wilde, who was also regarded as a "fleshly" poet; Wilde was a big man and Bunthorne was supposed to be small, but the latter's monocle, velvet suit and white streak (like Diaghilev) in his hair aped Whistler's appearance. Grosvenor's first name was originally to be Algernon, like Swinburne, but was altered to Archibald. So the appearance of both poets was an amalgam of several aesthetic personalities.

The Colonel's patter song is a mine of contemporary reference, often meaningless today. A full list can be found in the annotated text; it includes tributes to the coolness of the surgeon, Sir Joseph Paget, the talents of Jullien the "eminent musico", who was a well-known conductor of the day: "the pathos of Paddy as rendered by Boucicault" refers to a popular playwright and librettist who used Irish themes. Sir Garnet Wolseley's courage is again praised as in *The Pirates of Penzance*. There was even a type of Sherlock Holmes in the person of the astute Polish detective Ignatius Pollacky.

The stereotyped characters are still present. Grossmith's bird-like Bunthorne was a mockery of the word "fleshly", while Barrington's more robust girth made Grosvenor's sinking into cheerful normality very credible. The sad love-lorn middle-aged lady is Lady Jane, with one of the most hilarious props of all time, a 'cello on which she is prone to accompany herself. Like many of Gilbert's other ladies of a certain age, her devotion to her love-object, Bunthorne, is unswerving.

Carte excelled himself in publicity by placing Whistler and Wilde (the latter with a daffodil in his buttonhole), in the front row on the first night. Afterwards Wilde wrote to Grossmith – "... you were amazing – but I did not know that you were more amazing than I". When *Patience* was performed in the USA, Wilde, who was on Carte's lecture books, was sent there on a tour, and sportingly supported many a performance, having first created a memorable scene at the New York customs. When asked if he had anything to declare, he replied "Nothing but my genius". Carte said, "Wilde has given it a fresh spirit and it has simply made him. His business is enormous."

Sullivan only started the orchestral scoring ten days before the performance, partly because he was struggling to finish *The Martyr of Antioch* for the Leeds Festival, and partly because he was loath to leave the sunshine and gambling of Nice. So, as usual, he had to work through the night to complete the score. Here again, he sentimentalizes Gilbert's savagery, as in Lady Jane's "Silvered is the raven hair", and the Duke of Dunstable's "Your maiden hearts". There is a new musical element – the harking back to an English folk song style in "Prithee pretty maiden" – which was to become more prominent in later operas. Though charming, the music does not match the scintillation and point of the libretto, and the orchestration is less inspired than usual. Contemporary critics thought that "I hear the soft note" was an echo of the 17th-century; but this preceded the advent of the scholarly Dr Fellowes.

There were eight encores on the first night and an enthusiastic press – "the most subtle and incisive of all the contributions to the exhaustive satire of aestheticism," said one critic. The jokes came so thick and fast that many were missed, but the rest were appreciated, and the *Daily News* liked the "absence of anything approaching coarseness or vulgarity". However, the *Illustrated Sporting and Dramatic News* maintained that "this mountain of combined genius and intelligence produced a – well, a tolerably large-sized rat".

Carte had always wanted to build a tailor-made theatre to house his new school of genuinely English comic opera. The partnership and the size of the audiences the operas were now attracting now made this a viable proposition. In October 1881, *Patience* moved to the completed Savoy Theatre, with its innovatory electric lighting.

SYNOPSIS

A chorus of lovesick maidens sing of their shared, but unrequited, passion for the poet Reginald Bunthorne; they learn from the formidable Lady Jane that he loves the milkmaid Patience, who prefers her briskly heartwhole state to the languishing misery of the ladies' massed adoration ("I cannot tell what this love may be"). The Lady Angela warns of the advent of the maidens' erstwhile lovers, the 35th Dragoon Guards, who appear ("The soldiers of our Queen") led by Colonel Calverley who lists the ingredients of the "receipt of that popular mystery, Known to the world as a Heavy Dragoon" (as opposed to the Light Cavalry). The Duke of Dunstable compares his life, as the subject of unremitting sycophancy from all, to the relentless consumption of toffee.

Bunthorne enters, creatively rapt, with the attendant ladies, to the scorn of the dragoons ("Now is not this ridiculous"). In an aside he reveals that his poetic absorption is only skin-deep, but nevertheless reads aloud his "wild weird fleshly thing" entitled "Hollow! Hollow! Hollow!" (The practical Patience wonders if it is to be a hunting song!) The maidens trail away, having contemptuously dismissed the dragoons in their primary coloured uniforms as hopelessly unaesthetic. The bewildered Colonel cannot understand why his uniform no longer entrances the maidens ("when I first put this uniform on").

Left alone, Bunthorne describes how he has become a convincing "aesthetic sham" ("If you're anxious for to shine in the high aesthetic line"). He frightens Patience with his ensuing declaration of love, but, encouraged by Lady Angela, she decides that she, too, must try to experience this universal emotion. She recollects her childish affection for a boy playmate in the ensuing duet ("Long years ago, fourteen maybe"). Grosvenor promptly enters and de-

"Silvered is the raven hair". The formidable Alice Barnett, pictured with her 'cello, which was an indispensable prop for her Act II aria. Sullivan wrote a virtuoso 'cello obligato for this, which some Lady Janes have actually played on stage (above).

"*It's clear that medieval art alone retains its zest. To charm and please its devotees, we've done our level best*". The dragoon trio – Colonel Calverley, Major Murgatroyd and Lieutenant the Duke of Dunstable – attempt an aesthetic transformation to win back the affections of the maidens (Act II). This is a photograph of the 1907 revival (right).

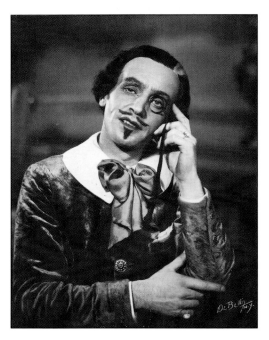

"*Then let me own, I'm an aesthetic sham!*" Martyn Green first played Bunthorne in 1934. His inspired antics, particularly in the Act II duets with Lady Jane and Grosvenor, are still remembered vividly by diehard Savoyards (above).

clares his love for her ("Prithee, pretty maiden"), explaining that he is not only her childhood friend, but also a poet. Patience is happy until she realises that the love she is feeling is not the suffering and selfless emotion that she has been led to believe is the only form of acceptable passion. Therefore it cannot be true love – so she renounces Grosvenor.

The discomforted dragoons confront Bunthorne, now tethered to his admirers by flower garlands, and ask him how he is going to wed all the ladies. He explains that on his solicitor's advice he has put himself up for raffle. Despite the dragoons' pleas, the maidens rush to purchase raffle tickets; they are interrupted by a distraught Patience who begs Bunthorne to take her as his bride. He agrees with alacrity. The rejected maidens miraculously "hear the soft note of the echoing voice Of an old, old love, long dead" and embrace the dragoons. Their defection is only temporary, for Grosvenor introduces himself as a rival to Bunthorne, and is immediately surrounded by revived rapturous maidens. While Patience confesses her unselfish love for Bunthorne, Grosvenor agonizes over the havoc caused by his attractiveness, and Bunthorne expresses his jealousy for Grosvenor in a complex ensemble.

Act II opens with the formidable Lady Jane, leaning pensively on a 'cello, lamenting the inevitable waning of feminine charms ("Silvered is the raven hair"). Grosvenor, à la Bunthorne, enters surrounded by the yearning maidens and recites his poetic effusion – it is of a more earthy nature than his rival's, but inspires a similar admiring reaction. He describes in the fable of "The Magnet and the

Churn" his hopeless love for Patience, and the maidens depart. Patience is clearly moved by his ensuing reaffirmation of devotion, but determined to remain true to her unselfish love of Bunthorne, despite his ungraciousness ("Love is a plaintive thing"). On her departure Lady Jane swears continuing allegiance to Bunthorne despite the desertion of the rest of the ladies and agrees to help him defeat Grosvenor ("So go to him and say to him"). The Major, Duke and Colonel, startlingly transformed into novice aesthetes, are aware of their imperfections ("It's clear that mediaeval art alone retains its zest"), but the Ladies Angela and Saphir are impressed enough with their efforts to consider dancing off with them ("If Saphir I choose to marry").

Grosvenor wishes, as he gazes narcissistically at himself in a mirror, that he could escape the maidens' attentions. The jealous Bunthorne threatens to curse Grosvenor unless he becomes commonplace in appearance, so that he is no longer adored. The relieved Grosvenor obliges and they both cheerfully anticipate a future in which Bunthorne will be reinstated on his pedestal and Grosvenor will be a "jolly Bank-holiday Everyday young man". As they dance round the stage, Patience enters to be stunned by Bunthorne's new amiability but, equally quickly, realizes it would be selfish to love such a pleasantly reformed character. Grosvenor's new ordinariness makes him unworthy of her affection, and therefore a totally suitable candidate for Patience's self-sacrificing love. Bunthorne, appalled, is reconciled to the prospect of Lady Jane as partner, but even this is denied him by the Duke, who determines to choose as a bride the one lady "who has the misfortune to be distinctly plain". In one of Gilbert's highly condensed final reshuffles, Saphir and the Colonel and Angela and the Major pair off happily, while Bunthorne is left "affectionately" contemplating a lily.

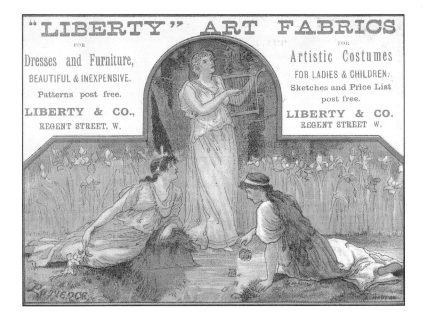

A*s far as costume was concerned, Patience was not too far removed from the reality of its times, as this Liberty advertisement shows (left).*

T*he cover of the 1937 Leeds programme features a more elegant Lady Jane (above).*

IOLANTHE

OR THE PEER AND THE PERI
SAVOY THEATRE (25 NOVEMBER 1882) 400 PERFORMANCES

DRAMATIS PERSONAE

THE LORD CHANCELLOR .... MR GEORGE GROSSMITH

EARL OF MOUNTARARAT .... MR RUTLAND BARRINGTON

EARL TOLLOLLER .... MR DURWARD LELY

PRIVATE WILLIS, *of the Grenadier Guards* .... MR MANNERS

STREPHON, *An Arcadian Shepherd* .... MR R TEMPLE

QUEEN OF THE FAIRIES .... MISS ALICE BARNETT

IOLANTHE, *A Fairy, Strephon's Mother* .... MISS JESSIE BOND

CELIA, *Fairy* .... MISS FORTESCUE

LEILA, *Fairy* .... MISS JULIA GWYNNE

FLETA, *Fairy* .... MISS SYBIL GREY

PHYLLIS, *An Arcadian Shepherdess and Ward in Chancery* .... MISS LEONORA BRAHAM

CHORUS OF DUKES, MARQUISES, EARLS, VISCOUNTS, BARONS AND FAIRIES

ACT I – An Arcadian Landscape

ACT II – Palace Yard, Westminster

DATE – Between 1700 and 1882

PIRATING was still very much on Carte's mind before the première of *Iolanthe*, for he had lost the legal battle in which he had tried to prevent American pirating of the previous operas. The rehearsals of *Iolanthe* were therefore held in secret, and for further security, the opera and its eponymous heroine were called *Perola*. The cast had to adjust to saying or singing four, instead of three, syllables just before the first night, when Gilbert announced the change of name.

Fairies were popular at this time; Hans Anderson was much admired, and dance and pantomime frequently contained a fairy element. Gilbert, that inveterate self-borrower, remembered his *Bab Ballad, the Fairy Curate*, with its half-human half-fairy hero, and one of his plays, *The Happy Land*, was about politicians and "peris". He took these ingredients and considered how he could use them to satirize the House of Lords at a time when Parliamentary reform was a topical issue. His other permanent preoccupation – worth versus birth – is again a major theme; the peers are horrified that membership of the Lords could be "thrown open to competitive examination", while true worth is already present in their sentry box in Palace Yard in the shape of the redoubtable Private Willis. Gilbert was also beginning to be uneasily aware of the implications of the women's movement, and, although the fairies do defeat the peers, the latter are made equal to them in their wing-sprouting assumption of fairyhood at the end.

Only a Gilbert could wave a fairy wand to incorporate his favourite role types in these disparate elements. Of all his middle-aged ladies, the Queen of the Fairies is the most impressive and least laughable in her infatuation – a truly rounded character in all senses of the word! The Lord Chancellor, too, is sympathetic – his reunion with Iolanthe is touching. His Nightmare song, incidentally, needs even more clarity and stamina than the patter songs of his lineal predecessors, Sir Joseph Porter and Major-General Stanley.

There are many references to the current political scene – for instance, the Queen of the Fairies attacks the Friday night custom of introducing a peer's bill. Many contemporary figures are thought to have been identified. Strephon is Lord Randolph Churchill, the Queen of the Fairies is obviously Victoria, the Lord Chancellor is Gladstone and Private Willis is Victoria's trusted ghillie John Brown. What Victoria said about this is not known.

As always, the production was detailed. Gilbert loved uniforms, so the peers' costumes by Wilhelm were splendid and correct in their assignation of the differing emblems of rank. One reviewer was particularly struck by the heading of the peers' procession by the Band of the Grenadier Guards. The scenery by Emden was very precise, too, in its reproductions of Westminster.

Sullivan was shattered by grief when he started work on the music, for his beloved mother had just died that May. Lady Molesworth invited him to stay on her magnificent Cornish estate at

"O *foolish fay". Alice Barnett made a suitably Wagnerian Fairy Queen in the 1882 première of Iolanthe. (top).*

"W *ith humbled breast". Sentenced to banishment for life for the crime of marrying a mortal, Iolanthe is eventually pardoned by the Fairy Queen. (above).*

Pencarrow and it was there that he composed the bulk of the opera. There has been a great deal written about Wagnerian similarities in *Iolanthe*, but they are exaggerated. The supposed leitmotiv of the Iolanthe call, the "Rhinemaiden" wailing of the fairies, the downward scale of the Chancellor's fugato entry as a cheerful version of Wotan's spear motiv are all merely mottoes and are not developed or metamorphosed in the true Wagnerian manner. Admittedly Alice Barnett, resplendent in breastplate and helmet as the Queen, had the unmistakable Valkyrie aura. But the ghost of Mendelssohn is always present in the exquisitely light and imaginative woodwind writing and the Midsummer Night's Dream atmosphere.

From now on, Savoy first nights were to be gala occasions. The Prince of Wales and Gladstone attended one of the early performances and must have admired the electric lights illuminating each fairy headdress and wand. Captain Shaw, chief of the London Fire Brigade, was also there (no doubt placed strategically in the front stalls by Carte), and the Queen begged him directly to quench her amorous flames with his "cold cascade": this had a double meaning as the gallant Captain concerned had also been the subject of Society gossip about his affair with the wife of Lord Colin Campbell! Sullivan was his normal genial and magnetic self, even though he had just heard that Edward Hall, his stockbroker, had gone bankrupt, so losing the composer £7,000, his total savings. Fortunately the opera was such a success that he was soon to recoup the loss.

Many critics felt that *Iolanthe* was the best opera yet; "the book and the setting appear to be one and indivisible" felt the critic of *Theatre*. Gladstone himself wrote a note of congratulation, appreciating "the manner in which the comic strain of the piece was blended with its harmonies of sight and sound so good in taste and so admirable in execution from beginning to end". However, there were two dissenting voices; *The Stage* predicted gloomily "It

"*When I went to the bar as a very young man*". The Lord Chancellor is one of Gilbert's most endearing comic creations.

"*Tripping hither, tripping thither*". The opening fairy chorus.

"*On fire that glows with heat intense*". The Fairy Queen wrestles successfully to suppress her affection for Private Willis in Act II. (above).

will not last ... the music is not tuneful enough to become popular", and *The People* objected to the political satire, accusing Gilbert of "bringing Truth and Love and Friendship into contempt, just as we are taught the devil does ... in the Gilbertian world there are no martyrs, no patriots and no lovers". How Gilbert would have enjoyed dressing up in horns and tail!

Five months later Sullivan was knighted. No such honour was offered to Gilbert – he had to wait until a different reign. Perhaps Queen Victoria was not amused.

SYNOPSIS

A chorus of bored fairies "tripping hither, tripping thither" dance in a dilatory manner in an Arcadian landscape. Their revels have been dutiful, rather than pleasurable, since the 25-year-old banishment of their sister Iolanthe to the bottom of a frog-filled stream. They beg the Queen of the Fairies to forgive her for the sin of marrying a mortal. She relents and summons Iolanthe, and a meek vision appears, festooned with water weeds which fall magically from her as she receives her pardon. Iolanthe explains that she chose the stream for her exile to be near her son Strephon, now aged 24, a shepherd who is "a fairy down to the waist – but his legs are mortal". He duly enters ("Good morrow, good mother") and announces his impending marriage to Phyllis, a Ward of Chancery, in defiance of the Lord Chancellor, who disapproves of him. The Queen suggests that a Member of Parliament is a more suitable occupation than a shepherd, but Strephon is dubious. He feels his partial fairy status, of which Phyllis is ignorant, would lead to confusion of Tory and Radical ideals ("Down to the waist, I'm a Tory of the most determined description, but my legs are a couple of confounded Radicals"). The fairies bid him farewell and Phyllis enters

I*olanthe rises from the stream where she has been living "among the frogs" to be pardoned by the Fairy Queen*

A *D'Oyly Carte publicity poster features Iolanthe (above).*

("Good morrow, good lover"); they discuss the Chancellor's amorous intentions towards her as well as those of half the House of Lords, and exit vowing "none shall part us from each other".

The peers march in ("Loudly let the trumpet bray") and the Lord Chancellor bewails his susceptibility to his pretty wards ("The Law is the true embodiment"). He nobly waives his claim to Phyllis, who is ushered in by Lord Mountararat. She listens to his and Lord Tolloller's declarations of love ("Of all the young ladies I know") but prefers her humble station in life ("I'm very much pained to refuse"). To silence their pleas and to general consternation, she rushes into Strephon's arms as he conveniently enters. The Lord Chanceller turns to legal logic to forbid their marriage, and before departing sings of his devotion to legal duty ("When I went to the Bar as a very young man"). Iolanthe promises help to the weeping Strephon, but the tender scene is overheard and misinterpreted by Phyllis, with Mountararat and Tolloller. She challenges Strephon who protests that Iolanthe is his mother, but all naturally feel that Iolanthe's girlish appearance makes this a biological impossibility. Phyllis reproaches Strephon ("For riches and rank I do not long") and agrees to marry either Montararat or Tolloller – in her grief she does not have any preference. Strephon desperately calls on the fairies, who obediently reappear. The peers and fairies defy one another and the Queen, as "an influential fairy", proclaims that Strephon is to enter Parliament to launch a rousing attack on the age-old rights of the House of Lords, climaxing with the blasphemous suggestion that "a Duke's exalted station Be attainable by Competitive Examination". The conflict escalates, as peers and fairies threaten each other ("Our lordly style you shall not quench"), until the peers kneel begging for mercy and Phyllis faints into the arms of her two suitors.

Act II introduces the philosophical Private Willis on sentry duty in the Palace Yard, Westminster, musing on Nature's brilliance in ensuring that every child is born as "either a little Liberal, Or else a little Conservative!" The chorus of fairies celebrate, and the peers mourn Strephon's iconoclastic political career; Lords Mountararat and Tolloller contemplate the unthinkable future of a House of Lords composed of peers of intelligence ("When Britain really ruled the waves"). Leila and Celia, two of the leading fairies, are much taken by the two lords, but the Queen pleads with them to sacrifice their love – she admits her own predilection for Private Willis ("O foolish fay"), and asks for the chief of the Fire Brigade, Captain Shaw to quench her love. Phyllis appears and is begged by Tolloller and Mountararat to make her choice, both nobly deferring to the other ("Though p'raps I may incur your blame"). Phyllis' charms have given the Lord Chancellor bad nights; he reenters with his Nightmare song, the most taxing of all patter songs ("When you're lying awake with a dismal headache"). He is encouraged to plead his suit by Mountararat and Tolloller who feel "Faint heart

"If we're weak enough to tarry". Strephon and Phyliss decide to defy the Lord Chancellor and marry despite his disapproval. This photograph is of the 1977 production, with Linda-Anne Hutchinson as a somewhat sophisticated Phyllis, as make-up and wig indicate (left).

never won fair lady". Strephon and Phyllis meet and he convinces her that Iolanthe is his mother and a fairy, and they are joyously reconciled ("If we're weak enough to tarry"), to the approval of Iolanthe. But when they ask her to plead for them with the Lord Chancellor, Iolanthe confesses she cannot; he is her mortal husband ("and Strephon's father"), and the cause of her banishment. The Lord Chancellor enters, chortling over his logical detachment in deciding that he in truth can freely marry Phyllis, but Iolanthe, now veiled, pleads for the young couple ("He loves!") and eventually reveals herself to the Lord Chancellor, at which the fairies break into Rhinemaidenish wails at the prospect of her imminent death as a result of her sin. As the Queen raises her spear, the peers enter with Strephon; the fairies all admit to secret assumption of the rank of peeresses by marriage. The Lord Chancellor, as an experienced equity draughtsman, solves all by inserting "don't" into "every fairy shall die who marries a mortal". The Queen summons Private Willis to deliver her from her fate, and promptly makes him a fairy. Magically, wings spring from his – and then the peers' – shoulders, and they all fly away to fairyland

"Welcome now to Fairyland". The fairy chorus greets Iolanthe after her reprieve from her sentence of life-long banishment (Act I). She is about to reveal to them that she has given birth to and raised a half-fairy son – "he's a fairy down to the waist, but his legs are mortal" (above).

PRINCESS IDA

OR CASTLE ADAMANT
SAVOY THEATRE (5 JANUARY 1884) 246 PERFORMANCES

DRAMATIS PERSONAE

KING HILDEBRAND .... MR RUTLAND BARRINGTON

HILARION, *His Son* .... MR H BRACY

CYRIL, *Hilarion's Friend* .... MR DURWARD LELY

FLORIAN, *Hilarion's Friend* .... MR RYLEY

KING GAMA .... MR GEORGE GROSSMITH

ARAC, *His Son* .... MR RICHARD TEMPLE

GURON, *His Son* .... MR LUGG

SCYNTHIUS, *His Son* .... MR W GREY

PRINCESS IDA, *Gama's Daughter* .... MISS LEONORA BRAHAM

LADY BLANCHE, *Professor of Abstract Science* .... MISS BRANDRAM

LADY PSYCHE, *Professor of Humanities* .... MISS CHARD

MELISSA, *Lady Blanche's Daughter* .... MISS JESSIE BOND

SACHARISSA, *Girl Graduate* .... MISS SYBIL GREY

CHLOE, *Girl Graduate* .... MISS HEATHCOTE

ADA, *Girl Graduate* .... MISS TWYMAN

SOLDIERS, COURTIERS, "GIRL GRADUATES", "DAUGHTERS OF THE PLOUGH", &c

---

ACT I – Pavilion in King Hildebrand's Palace

ACT II – Gardens of Castle Adamant

ACT III – Courtyard of Castle Adamant

ON 8 FEBRUARY 1883, Sullivan, Carte and Gilbert had signed an agreement for a period of five years, in which composer and librettist were each assigned a third of the takings after expenses had been deducted – a significant factor in the future "carpet quarrel". In return, Carte was empowered to insist on the production of a new work at six months notice. Gilbert's agreement was understandable, but Sullivan's incomprehensible, in view of his commitments to the Leeds Festival in particular, to serious composition in general and to the lure of the gambling tables. Allied to this was his increasing dislike of this genre of composing.

So a new opera was needed, although *Iolanthe* was still running successfully. Gilbert's first thought was to press Sullivan to set his "magic lozenge" plot, in which, by swallowing a magic lozenge, a character could be changed into another. Sullivan rightly pointed out that this theme had already been explored in *The Sorcerer,* and moreover that the idea was too complicated and artificial. Gilbert capitulated.

Since *Iolanthe*, the subject of feminine emancipation must have been on Gilbert's mind, though not for the first time, for in 1870 he had made a "per-version" of Tennyson's expansive verse-play, *The Princess*. Gilbert had conceived this as a burlesque, so the music was comprised of well-known songs from popular opera composers of the day, like Offenbach or Hervé. In the following decade, the first women's university colleges (Girton in 1869 and Newnham in 1871) had been founded, and women's education was generally improving. Gilbert was distrustful of this new emancipation, though he was to make Ida's stubborn courage sympathetically dotty. There are other echoes – of Thackeray's *The Rose and the Ring,* and the plot of Rossini's *Le Comte Ory,* for instance. When he produced an outline of this new plot, Sullivan rather reluctantly agreed to set it.

The blank verse is well-managed and often sonorous, with some intellectual punning that must have gone over the contemporary audience's head; they were unlikely to be familiar enough with Macbeth to recognise this allusion:

"Why these ...
Are men she would have added, but 'are men'
Stuck in her throat!"

But unexpectedly the proportions are clumsy. Gilbert converted the original Prologue into Act I and renumbered the other acts. Together, Acts I and III were only half the length of Act II. The review in *Figaro* pointed out that the action dragged and overall the piece was too long (possibly because Gilbert had used many of the original speeches, but condensed the action).

The characters, however, are less stereotyped than is sometimes the case, while Gilbert openly admitted there was something of himself in King Gama. He even quoted the king's "Everybody

"Yet everybody says I'm such a disagreeable man!" John Reed as King Gama, Princess Ida's father. The date of the photograph is uncertain, but he is wearing the 1954 revival costume. Gilbert recognizes that he resembled Gama in some of his own personal characteristics, but, like Gama, could not "think why" some people found him disagreeable (above).

"For a month to dwell". Arac, Guron and Scynthius, Gama's three sons, though doughty fighting men, themselves admit that, "on the whole", they are "not intelligent". They also lose their duel with Hilarion, Cyril and Florian (above).

says I'm such a disagreeable man! And I can't think why" at a dinner many years later. Lady Blanche is one of his most unpleasant older ladies, with a lust for power rather than for any weak-kneed male. But the three thick-headed sons of Gama rank with the police in *The Pirates of Penzance* for sheer lovable cowardice coupled with ruefully practical acceptance of the exigiencies of combat.

There are various topical references. Ida in her Act I speech mentions Swan and Edgar and similar fashionable stores of the day, whose names were as indivisible as those of Gilbert and Sullivan: many of these lines have been cut recently, or altered as irrelevant. The theme of "Darwinian man" was still an important religious, as well as scientific, issue at the time; *The Origin of Species* had created a public furor on its publication in 1859 and its reverberations were still being felt, as demonstrated in the conclusion of Lady Psyche's song the "Ape and the Lady" that "Darwinian man, though well-behaved, At best is only a monkey shaved".

The rehearsals were coloured by Gilbert's painful gout, which turned his normally irascible cajoling into rank bad temper, especially with poor Grossmith who took to injecting himself with drugs. He hated both his minor role as Gama and the blank verse idiom, complaining that he had been made to feel a "perfect fool". Another actor is reported to have said he wouldn't be bullied – "I know my lines" he said. "That may be so, but you don't know mine," Gilbert lashed back.

The first night was nearly a disaster. Sullivan's old kidney problem had returned, and Cellier was prepared to deputize. However, stiffened by morphine and black coffee, the composer somehow hoisted himself onto the rostrum, conducted magnificently and promptly fainted after the performance. In addition there was much unwanted mirth from the gallery; Gilbert had not realised that Ida's simulated watery dive onto a backstage mattress would be visible to the galleryites. Gilbert, instead of nervously absenting himself from the theatre as was his practice, remained backstage in view of Sullivan's illness, ostensibly reading a newspaper. The French stage armourer announced joyously that the première was a success and Gilbert growled bearishly "I suppose he expected to see me kissing all the carpenters".

Sullivan had delayed composing the music. He would never shelve personal responsibilities; to his sorrow Frederic Clay had just died suddenly, while his beloved brother's widow and her family were emigrating to California. Despite these personal preoccupations, *Princess Ida* is one of Sullivan's best scores. There is a fine example of his madrigal style in "The world is but a broken toy", and some splendid Handelian parody, especially in the songs of Gama's sons ("This helmet I suppose", and "We are warriors three"), where the orchestration is particularly witty. The stolidly spaced chords in the Act II trio "We may remark" brilliantly reflect mindless truculence. But in Ida's "I built upon a rock" he strayed into a true grand opera style, and an article in *Truth* perspicaciously suggested that it was the "right music in the wrong place". The reviews agreed that the music was Sullivan's best "in every way ... apart from his serious works" *The Saturday Review* admired the "distinct drollery" of the scoring.

All these opinions, plus encouragement from the most musically knowledgeable of his friends, convinced Sullivan that he was capable of more significant musical achievements than the stimulus of Gilbert's libretti could provide. The root of the quarrels that were to dog the partnership in future lay, not in their superficial petty causes, but in this deep-rooted dichotomy of aim.

"For I'm a peppery kind of king". Richard Watson, an Australian Savoyard, played King Hildebrand in the 1932 revival. He certainly looks as if he is not in the mood to stand any nonsense from Gama or Princess Ida herself (above).

SYNOPSIS

In front of King Hildebrand's palace, a chorus of his soldiers and courtiers, including his son Hilarion's friends, Cyril and Florian, anxiously scan the panorama for a sight of the retinue of King Gama. The latter is due to bring his daughter, Princess Ida, to join Prince Hilarion, to whom she was married when they were both babies. Gama appears in the distance but without Ida, and the chorus and Hildebrand threaten dire reprisal if Gama is not true to his word. Hilarion speculates on how the princess must have

"*Expressive glances shall be our lances*". Hilarion is confident that, despite what Gama tells him about Princess Ida's determination to live a life without men, he has the power to overcome her resistance. John Fryatt is seen as Hilarion (above)

Leonard Osborn as Cyril and Fisher Morgan as King Hildebrand in the 1954 revival (below right).

changed in the 20 years since he saw her, especially as he has heard that she has foresworn the world and devoted herself to learning. Gama's three doltish sons, Arac, Guron and Scynthius appear ("We are warriors three"). Gama introduces himself ("If you give me your attention"), and proceeds to be determinedly rude to everyone in sight: he also describes Ida's women's university with its hundred students. He grudgingly admits that if Hildebrand addresses her "most politely" she might relent. Hildebrand keeps Gama and his sons as hostages, threatening them with hanging should Hilarion disappear. Hilarion and his friends Cyril and Florian look forward to their encounter with Ida ("Expressive glances"). Gama and the sons return, shackled, and bemoan their fate.

Act II opens with the girl students of Castle Adamant are seated at Lady Psyche's feet discussing Man, "Nature's sole mistake". Lady Blanche's list of expulsions and punishments and Ida's aria ("At this my call") both ridicule feminist ideals.

Hilarion, Cyril and Florian "Gently, gently" appear at the foot of the castle walls. Hilarion patronisingly mocks the apparent unattainability of the university's scholastic aims ("They intend to send a wire"), and they disguise themselves as students in some conveniently available college robes ("I am a maiden, cold and stately"). Princess Ida appears and admits her new students, and they forswear the world as a "broken toy", as she exits. Lady Psyche, however, recognises Florian as her brother and introduces him to Melissa, Lady Blanche's sympathetic daughter; all five confess that Ida's views are perhaps somewhat one-sided ("The woman of the wisest wit"). Lady Blanche realises that the new students are male, but her cooperation is ensured when Melissa points out that Blanche could be head of the university if Ida were restored to her husband.

A disastrous picnic lunch with the new students ensues, in

which Cyril becomes tipsy and sings a kissing song, is punched by Hilarion and all is discovered. Ida, in fleeing, falls into the river and Hilarion promptly saves her to the joy of the chorus. Ida, though wet, is undeterred, and orders all three men to be chained and bound, despite Hilarion's enamoured plea "Whom thou has chained". As they are marched away, Melissa announces the storming of the castle walls by Hildebrand's soldiers, and they soon appear, accompanied by the ladies' lamentations. Hildebrand puts his case ("Some years ago"), reinforced by the truculent trio of Ida's brothers, who will be slain if Hildebrand is denied his rights. Ida, however, hurls defiance at the intruders.

Act III starts with the ladies in defiant mood ("Death to the invader"), but their courage is only skin-deep, as Melissa confesses ("Thus our courage all untarnished"). Ida fails to rally her forces and, disillusioned ("I built upon a rock"), admits to herself that she, too, is afraid. An unnerved Gama appears, temporarily freed. Hildebrand has devised for him the unique torture of solicitous care and hospitality, and constant turning of the other cheek ("Whene'er I spoke Sarcastic joke"). Gama begs Ida to agree to open the gates; the chorus of soldiers enter ("When anger spreads his wing"), and he encounters Hilarion, Florian and Cyril in their women's clothes, taunting them until they agree to a duel with his three sons, who find their armour somewhat oppressive ("This helmet I suppose"). However, as Hilarion and his friends triumph, the Princess yields.

Barbara Lilley as Princess Ida (left), Jane Metcalfe as Melissa (centre) and Julia Goss as Lady Psyche (right) review the current state of affairs at her "women's university" (above).

THE MIKADO

OR THE TOWN OF TITIPU
SAVOY THEATRE (14 MARCH 1885) 672 PERFORMANCES

DRAMATIS PERSONAE

THE MIKADO OF JAPAN .... MR R TEMPLE

NANKI-POO, *His Son, Disguised as a Wandering Minstrel,*
and in Love with Yum-Yum .... MR DURWARD LELY

KO-KO, *Lord High Executioner of Titipu* .... MR GEORGE GROSSMITH

POOH-BAH, *Lord High Everything Else* .... MR RUTLAND BARRINGTON

PISH-TUSH, *A Noble Lord* .... MR FREDERICK BOVILL

YUM-YUM, *One of Three Sisters – Wards of Ko-Ko* .... MISS LEONORA BRAHAM

PITTI-SING, *One of Three Sisters – Wards of Ko-Ko* .... MISS JESSIE BOND

PEEP-BO, *One of Three Sisters – Wards of Ko-Ko* .... MISS SYBIL GREY

KATISHA, *An Elderly Lady, in Love with Nanki-Poo* .... MISS ROSINA BRANDRAM

CHORUS OF SCHOOL-GIRLS, NOBLES, GUARDS AND COOLIES

ACT I – Court-yard of Ko-Ko's Official Residence

ACT II – Ko-Ko's Garden

WHILE Princess Ida was lurching uncomfortably through its run, Sullivan dropped a bombshell, announcing "it is impossible for me to do another piece of the character of those already written by Gilbert". Gilbert correctly pointed out that this refusal would break the contract between the triumvirate, but the normally easy-going Sullivan stuck to his point, explaining that, because of the demands of the libretto, he constantly suppressed his natural desire for the music to "arise and speak for itself". He felt that his scores were becoming stale and derivative, and that he wanted a real human situation where the music would "intensify the emotional element not only of the actual words but of the situation". But he hoped "with all my heart that there may be no break in our chain of joint workmanship". Unfortunately, Gilbert's immediate reaction was to produce another "Magic Lozenge" libretto, which Sullivan firmly rejected. Gilbert, smarting, refused to construct another plot and Sullivan accepted his decision.

The result of this exchange was impasse: each man felt that the other minimized his contribution, yet both men instinctively knew that it was only when they worked in tandem that they were at their mutual best. Soon after this, however – though the incident has been considered apocryphal by some – a ceremonial Japanese sword that hung on Gilbert's library wall fell down to sever temporarily his obsession with his beloved "Lozenge". It reminded him that things Japanese were all the vogue – there was a complete Japanese exhibition "village" in Knightsbridge and its buildings, fabrics, furniture and, above all, the alien and exotic manners and customs of its unfamiliar inhabitants all being much admired. So why not a Japanese subject, blissfully free of lozenges or potions?

What Gilbert finally produced, hidden under a Japanese parasol, was one of his most universal and telling satires on petty bureaucracy and nepotism. Sullivan duly voiced his "inexpressible relief" and appropriately, on the opening night, Ko-Ko staggered on stage carrying Gilbert's inspirational sword.

The plot hung on its Japanese clichés – respect for the mighty and worship of the sun and moon, coupled with horrific tortures and savagery, as exemplified in much of Japanese national traditions and art. The emphasis on the crime of "flirting" possibly arose from a suppressed interest in Japanese erotica, according to Jefferson. The Japanese words used in the remonstrances and silencing of Katisha in the Act I finale "O ni! bikkuri shakkuri to!" has had many translations, but the literal one "surprise, with a hiccup" seems to fit the situation very neatly. The words at the Mikado's entrance, "Miya sama" are from a contemporary Japanese war song, dating from 1868. Though rather more adventurous translations have been offered, Bailey's version, an innocuous verse about princes, Imperial chargers and chastisement of rebels, seems generally accepted.

Gilbert, with his insistence on verisimilitude, ordered the girls' dresses from Liberty's oriental silks department. He used a magni-

"Behold the Lord High Executioner!" Ko-Ko, the humble tailor who is unexpectedly reprieved from his sentence of death for flirting and enobled as Titipu's Lord High Executioner, is undoubtedly Gilbert and Sullivan's best-loved character, just as The Mikado is their most popular opera (above).

"So please you, sir, we much regret". Yum-Yum and her two sisters apologize in song to Pooh-Bah, Lord High Everything Else, for their unintentional rudeness to a man of such high rank. Kenneth Sandford is Pooh-Bah (top).

"The flowers that bloom in the spring". A pensive Ko-Ko reflects that these "have nothing to do with the case", faced, as he is, with the prospect of marriage to "a most unattractive old thing... With a caricature of a face" (above).

ficent gold-embroidered replica of the official costume for the Mikado, and found an equally resplendent 200-year-old affair for Katisha. He engaged the services of a geisha girl from the Knightsbridge Exhibition to teach Japanese deportment to the girls. Despite her linguistic limitations – all she could say was "Sixpence please", the price of a cup of tea in the "village" – she drilled them in the ancient feminine arts of hissing, giggling and snapping of fans open and shut which have all become an inseparable part of *The Mikado* performance tradition.

The characters were tailor-made for the established Savoy cast. The names of Pooh-Bah and Pish-Tush come from a *Bab Ballad King Borria Bungalee Boo*. Gilbert's apprenticeship in pantomime gave him the idea of Pooh-Bah's job-multiplicity as Lord High Everything Else: it is based on the character Lord Factotum, from Planché's *The Sleeping Beauty*, produced in 1840. Further pantomime elements are obvious – Nanki-Poo can easily be played as a principal boy, the Mikado as a demon king and Katisha by a man as a pantomime dame. She is one of the most bloodthirsty of Gilbert's middle-aged ladies, but, in some ways, the most vulnerable under her arrogantly savage veneer.

Though Gilbert does not concentrate on a single specific satirical theme, there are numerous shafts at contemporary customs – Ko-Ko's "little list" and the Mikado's objects of ire are almost a Victorian social history in themselves. For instance, the Mikado's "parliamentary trains" had to serve every station in the land daily by law, while the "Monday Pops" were weekly forerunners of the Proms, organised by Chappells, the music publishers. In the first performances, Ko-Ko mocked current political figures by donning a

Gladstone collar, a Salisbury beard and Chamberlain's monocle and orchid buttonhole. There is an interesting comment on the exploration of Africa in the references to the Congo and the Niger in "There's beauty in the bellow of the blast" – for this was the decade of Stanley's "Dr Livingstone I presume?"

The rehearsals were tense. Gilbert bullied Grossmith constantly, but was still open to hints on the text. For instance, Lely said "rapture" in too exaggerated a manner; "modified rapture" growled Gilbert. Lely dutifully echoed him, and so it remained. The first night was traumatic, as poor Grossmith had been so browbeaten that he was very tense, and had many memory lapses; but gradually his natural high spirits bubbled up, especially after an inadvertent stumble in "The flowers that bloom in the spring" at which the audience laughed, and he began his usual inspired antics (Sullivan later admitted that Grossmith's nervousness had "nearly upset the piece"). Gilbert threatened to cut the Mikado's song just before the

"Mercy, even for Pooh-Bah!" The "more humane" Mikado has just revealed to the hapless Ko-Ko, Pitti-Sing and Pooh-Bah the punishment for the unwitting execution of his son and heir, Nanki-Poo – "something lingering, with boiling oil in it" (above).

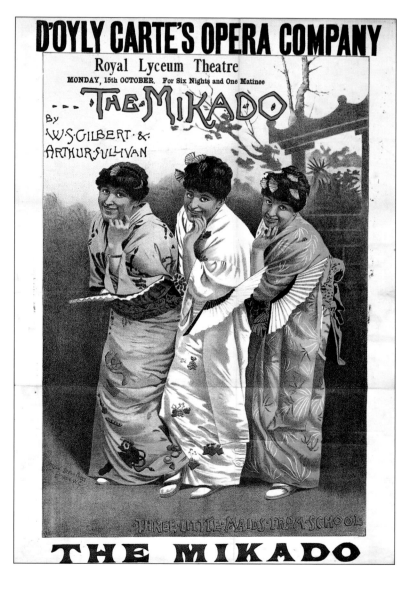

"Three little maids from school are we". Yum-Yum and her two sisters arrive on the scene (left).

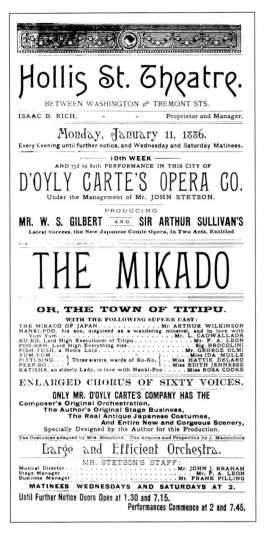

Hollis St. Theatre.

BETWEEN WASHINGTON AND TREMONT STS.

ISAAC B. RICH, - - Proprietor and Manager.

Monday, January 11, 1886.

Every Evening until further notice, and Wednesday and Saturday Matinees.

——— 10th WEEK ———

AND 73d to 80th PERFORMANCE IN THIS CITY OF

D'OYLY CARTE'S OPERA CO.

Under the Management of Mr. JOHN STETSON.

PRODUCING

MR. W. S. GILBERT AND SIR ARTHUR SULLIVAN'S

Latest Success, the New Japanese Comic Opera, In Two Acts, Entitled

THE MIKADO

OR, THE TOWN OF TITIPU.

WITH THE FOLLOWING SUPERB CAST:

THE MIKADO OF JAPAN . . . . Mr. ARTHUR WILKINSON
NANKI-POO, his son, disguised as a wandering minstrel, and in love with
Yum Yum . . . . Mr. L. CADWALLADR
KO-KO, Lord High Executioner of Titipu . . . . Mr. F. A. LEON
POO-BAH, Lord High Everything else . . . . Sig. BROCOLINI
PISH-TUSH, a Noble Lord . . . . Mr. GEORGE OLMI
YUM-YUM. . . . . Miss IDA MULLE
PITTI-SING. . . . } Three sisters, wards of Ko-Ko, } . . Miss HATTIE DELARO
PEEP-BO. . . . . } . . Miss EDITH JENNESSE
KATISHA, an elderly Lady, in love with Nanki-Poo . . . . . Miss ROSA COOKE

ENLARGED CHORUS OF SIXTY VOICES.

ONLY MR. D'OYLY CARTE'S COMPANY HAS THE
Composer's Original Orchestration,
The Author's Original Stage Business,
The Real Antique Japanese Costumes,
And Entire New and Gorgeous Scenery,
Specially Designed by the Author for this Production.

The Costumes adapted by Mrs. Shepherd. The Armors and Properties by J. Macnichols

Large and Efficient Orchestra.

MR. STETSON'S STAFF:

Musical Director . . . . Mr. JOHN J. BRAHAM
Stage Manager . . . . Mr. F. A. LEON
Business Manager . . . . Mr. FRANK PILLING

MATINEES WEDNESDAYS AND SATURDAYS AT 2.

Until Further Notice Doors Open at 1.30 and 7.15.

Performances Commence at 2 and 7.45.

A *playbill for the 1886 American production of The Mikado. Note the reasons for authenticity the playbill features (above).*

T*he sky darkens, as Katisha calls for vengeance at the end of Act I (far right top).*

D*onald Adams, one of the great Mikados of modern times, started playing the part in 1953 (far right bottom).*

rise of the curtain, but the cast begged for its retention, and the original position of "The sun whose rays" after "Three little maids" was altered because Yum-Yum became too breathless.

Though Sullivan used a pentatonic Japanese tune for the entry of the Mikado, the rest of the music could not be more English. He still appears influenced by Mendelssohn, by Mozart (the contrapuntal trio in Act I mentioned below has often been compared to the Osmin, Pedrillo and Belmonte trio in *Die Entführung aus dem Serail*) and by Schubert. However his ballad style seemed to grow from the relaxed, mellifluous melodic line of 18th-century composers like Arne, Dibden or Boyce, though the charming rhythmic hesitancies and unexpected modulations are all his own in "The sun whose rays", where he uses a "pedal" or drone bass to support a particularly expressive vocal line. As in so many of the later operas, there is a ballett type of madrigal "Brightly dawns our wedding day," which bypasses the previous centuries and derives from Thomas Morley. Sullivan further exhibits his musical scholarship in the apposite quotation of the Bach "Great" G minor organ fugue subject in the bass line under "Bach interwoven with Spohr and Beethoven" in the Mikado's song, and revels in his Bach-like contrapuntal skill in combining the three vocal lines in Ko-Ko, Pish-Tush and Pooh-Bah's Act I trio.

The use of woodwind, as always, is felicitous – the bassoon gurgles in "Three little maids", or the flute, clarinet and piccolo shrieks mimicking the criminal's cries in the execution description, add a witty commentary on the action. *The Mikado* is perhaps the richest musically of the Savoy operas – it does not possess the emotional depth of *The Yeomen of the Guard*, nor the reflection of current serious musical taste as in *Ruddigore, Princess Ida* or *Iolanthe*, but is, paradoxically, written in the purest English vocal tradition.

The reviews agreed – "the whole thing is like a glass of champagne". The *Daily Telegraph* remarked ruefully that "we are all being more or less Japanned", and that "the most beautiful things in *The Mikado* come when the composer appeals rather to tears than to laughter". Gilbert was apparently somewhat ruffled by this. Though *Theatre* did notice the flippant treatment of violence, cowardice and selfishness, it conceded that "its author's rhyming and rhythmic gifts have never been more splendidly displayed" in "musical jewels of great price", and that the dialogue was "full of points and hits". The final accolade was a Royal Command performance at Balmoral some years later on 4 September 1891, after which Queen Victoria noted in her journal: "Though there were witty remarks and amusing topical allusions, the story is rather silly" – possibly the company's performance was less good than that of *The Gondoliers* which she preferred. But she admired the good looks of the chorus and George Thorne's Ko-Ko who "jumped about most wonderfully".

There was a determined attempt at American pirating by Duff, the manager of the Standard Theater, New York, because he was offended that the opera had been offered to Stetson and the Fifth Avenue Theater. So, with resourceful and melodramatic guile, D'Oyly Carte took over a touring company in secret, booking their sea passage under false names and calling himself Harry Chapman. After only two days' secret rehearsal, the American *Mikado* was presented on 19 August 1885. Its success led to the indefatigable Helen Lenoir arranging tours all over the USA and to Cellier's Australian tour. It has remained the most popular of all the Savoy operas.

SYNOPSIS

In a splendidly attitudinal chorus, the Japanese nobles of Titipu introduce themselves, followed by Nanki-Poo, a "Wandering minstrel", who sings a ballad to show the range of his wares. He is searching for Yum-Yum, whom he met a year ago and who reciprocated his immediate love for her, despite the disapproval of her guardian Ko-Ko, the local tailor, to whom she was already engaged. Nanki-Poo's quest began when he heard that Ko-Ko had been condemned to death for flirting, but Pish-Tush, one of the noblemen, tells of Ko-Ko's reprieve and elevation to the rank of Lord High Executioner. He sings of the Mikado's cruel condemnation of flirting ("Our great Mikado, virtuous man"). Pooh-Bah, the archetypal snob, sonorously enumerates his many official posts as Lord High Everything Else, and warns Nanki-Poo that Ko-Ko is to be married to Yum-Yum that very day.

Ko-Ko enters with due pomp, and recounts his dizzy rise to his present rank ("Taken from the county jail"), and describes his "little list" of society nuisances whom he would choose as his victims if he should ever have to act in his official capacity. He asks Pooh-Bah's advice in his various offices on the arrangements for his forthcoming wedding to Yum-Yum. She enters, with her sisters Peep-Bo and Pitti-Sing, plus a "train of little ladies" and they introduce themselves, tittering, with much provocative use of their fans, as "Three little maids from school". They greet Nanki-Poo with delight, then tease Pooh-Bah ("So please you, sir, we much regret"). Yum-Yum is left alone with Nanki-Poo, who reveals that he is the Mikado's son, but is disguised as a Second Trombone in the local band, thus evading the amorous pursuit of Katisha, an elderly lady from his father's court. "So, in spite of all temptation" they kiss each other. Ko-Ko is brought a letter from the Mikado complaining of the dearth of executions in Titipu and threatening to reduce the town to the level of a village unless one is carried out forthwith. As this will involve everyone "in irretrievable ruin", Pish-Tush and Pooh-Bah suggest that Ko-Ko might execute himself, but eventually agree that a substitute must be found – a role Pooh-Bah declines.

THE
D'OYLY CARTE
OPERA COMPANY

GILBERT & SULLIVAN

T*he original publicity poster for The Mikado. Note that here Ko-Ko wears spectacles (top).*

"T*he sun whose rays". Yum-Yum glories in her peerless beauty as a "child of Nature" (above).*

In the following trio, they sing (in triple counterpoint) of their multi-occupational predicaments, but all agree that "To sit in solemn silence in a dull dark dock" awaiting execution, is not a fate to be welcomed. Nanki-Poo, despairing of marrying Yum-Yum, decides to take his life, but agrees to be a volunteer victim, if he is allowed a month of marriage first. All rejoice, despite the temporary nature of the reprieve ("The threatened cloud has passed away"), but, at this point, Katisha erupts onto the scene, claiming the hand of Nanki-Poo ("Oh fool, that fleest My hallowed joys!"). The chorus maintain that "he's going to marry Yum-Yum" and Katisha attempts to announce Nanki-Poo's true identity, but is overwhelmed by the chorus and leaves, swearing vengeance.

In the opening scene of Act II, Yum-Yum is being dressed on her wedding-day and is admiring herself artlessly ("The sun whose rays are all ablaze"), but sobs as she is reminded of the shortness of her wedded bliss. She is comforted by Nanki-Poo, joined by Pitti-Sing and Pish-Tush ("Brightly dawns our wedding day"). Ko-Ko puts a stop to their somewhat enforced gaiety by his revelation of the Mikado's law that a wife has to be buried alive if her husband is beheaded, and Yum-Yum's passion consequently cools forthwith; all three commiserate with each other in "Here's a how-de-do". On hearing of the imminent approach of the Mikado, Ko-Ko panics at Nanki-Poo's demand for immediate execution (for the latter says he cannot live without Yum-Yum), and hastily bestows Yum-Yum upon Nanki-Poo, who removes her immediately.

The men's chorus enter to a march ("Miya sama, miya sama") and Katisha relishes her power as the Mikado's "daughter-in-law elect". He himself delivers lists of the punishments he has devised to fit sundry crimes ("A more humane Mikado never Did in Japan exist"). A gory, but fictional, account is given by Ko-Ko, Pitti-Sing and Pooh-Bah of the required execution that has just taken place ("The criminal cried as he dropped him down"), only to learn that the Mikado has merely come in search of his errant son, whose name appears on the execution certificate. They are promptly condemned to death by "something lingering, with boiling oil in it". In the ensuing glee, the Mikado, Katisha, Pooh Bah, Pitti-Sing and Ko-Ko philosophise on fate and happiness ("See how the Fates their gifts allot"). Nanki-Poo persuades Ko-Ko to consider marrying Katisha and both contemplate their existence under such circumstances ("The flowers that bloom in the Spring"). Katisha enters with such a despairing song ("Hearts do not break") that Ko-Ko is encouraged to woo her with his ballad about the touchingly suicidal "little tom-tit" who sat "On a tree by a river", and they romp off together in ill-assorted bliss ("There's beauty in the bellow of the blast"). They return to plead for mercy from the Mikado for Ko-Ko's presumed execution of Nanki-Poo, who enters with Yum-Yum to kneel in front of his father. All is pronounced satisfactory and the opera ends in general rejoicing.

RUDDIGORE

OR THE WITCH'S CURSE

SAVOY THEATRE (21 JANUARY 1887) 288 PERFORMANCES

DRAMATIS PERSONAE

— MORTALS —

ROBIN OAKAPPLE, *A Young Farmer* .... MR GEORGE GROSSMITH

RICHARD DAUNTLESS, *His Foster-Brother – a Man-o'-War's-Man* .... MR DURWARD LELY

SIR DESPARD MURGATROYD, *of Ruddygore – a Wicked Baronet* .... MR RUTLAND BARRINGTON

OLD ADAM GOODHEART, *Robin's Faithful Servant* .... MR RUDOLPH LEWIS

ROSE MAYBUD, *A Village Maiden* .... MISS LEONORA BRAHAM

MAD MARGARET .... MISS JESSIE BOND

DAME HANNAH, *Rose's Aunt* .... MISS ROSINA BRANDRAM

ZORAH, *Professional Bridesmaid* .... MISS JOSEPHINE FINDLAY

RUTH, *Professional Bridesmaid* .... MISS LINDSAY

— GHOSTS —

SIR RUPERT MURGATROYD, *The First Baronet* .... MR PRICE

SIR JASPER MURGATROYD, *The Third Baronet* .... MR CHARLES

SIR LIONEL MURGATROYD, *The Sixth Baronet* .... MR TREVOR

SIR CONRAD MURGATROYD, *The Twelfth Baronet* .... MR BURBANK

SIR DESMOND MURGATROYD, *The Sixteenth Baronet* .... MR TUER

SIR GILBERT MURGATROYD, *The Eighteenth Baronet* .... MR WILBRAHAM

SIR MERVYN MURGATROYD, *The Twentieth Baronet* .... MR COX

and

SIR RODERIC MURGATROYD, *The Twenty-first Baronet* .... MR RICHARD TEMPLE

CHORUS OF OFFICERS, ANCESTORS, AND PROFESSIONAL BRIDESMAIDS

ACT I – The Fishing Village of Rederring, in Cornwall

ACT II – Picture Gallery in Ruddygore Castle

TIME – Early in the Present Century

"*When the night wind howls*". *Sir Roderic features in this publicity poster (above).*

"*We're thoroughly tired of being admired*". *The bucks and blades of the Act I male chorus in the 1922 revival, for which a new overture was arranged by Geoffrey Toye (far right top).*

"*I know a youth*". *These illustrations of Robin and Rose come from the original programme for the 1887 production (far right bottom).*

AFTER the success of his new cantata *The Golden Legend* at the Leeds Festival in October 1886, Sullivan felt he had surpassed himself, though he was somewhat put out by Ethel Smythe's remark that she thought that *The Mikado* was his best composition. Serious music had therefore preoccupied Sullivan throughout the year, so he gave short shrift to Gilbert's overprompt re-submission of his "Lozenge" plot. Undeterred, Gilbert re-appeared with a version of his 1869 play, *Ages Ago*. Sullivan was reasonably taken with the idea of a melodrama burlesque with some side-glances at Hamlet and ghosts behaving like human beings, but perhaps it was sentimental memories of the two men's first meeting at one of the play's rehearsals that made him agree to set the new libretto.

The old melodramas stemmed from before the days of Gilbert's writing apprenticeship, but, though they were no longer fashionable, he felt they would be well enough remembered for his parody to be effective. This is the first opera which does not satirize a contemporary theme, but it does attack marriage, materialism and jingoism, especially in the ironic use of the Union Jack to ward off evil. There are few topical allusions, with one exception. Dick Dauntless' Act I shanty, whitewashing the retreat of a British cutter from a French frigate, and sneering at the "Darn'd Mounseer" and his foreign ways, nearly caused an international incident, insulting the Gallic honour upheld by the Parisian newspaper *Le Figaro*.

There are still topsy-turvy elements in the plot – Rose's unwitting engagement to a cad, and her constant switching of her amorous allegiance, while Mad Margaret and the evil Sir Despard are converted into twin pillars of conventional rectitude by the end of the opera. The view of human nature seems twisted and the mockery is rather cruel. For instance, Rose's good deeds are entirely inappropriate and useless to their recipients, and the general feeling is that we are all basically evil, and goodness merely superficial.

Sullivan had different ideals, and where Gilbert's words seem to require a rather savage mockery in the music, Sullivan set the words at their face value. For the first time the words and music did not seem to come from the same brain. Gilbert said there was too much music which held up the story and was not humorous enough. The ghost music, he felt, was "like introducing fifty lines of *Paradise Lost* into a farcical comedy". However when Lely, the first Dick Dauntless, introduced a little hornpipe at the end of his shanty, Gilbert kept it in the production.

Gilbert's fascination with uniform (he loved dressing up) ran riot when he dressed the 20 "bucks and blades" of the men's Act I chorus in as many different regimental uniforms of the Napoleonic Wars, which were all checked for authenticity by the Deputy Quartermaster–General on the staff of that old friend of the Savoy operas, Sir Garnet Wolseley. The cost of costumes and sets reached the astronomical figure of £8,000. As always, every detail was taken

into consideration, down to the illuminated glass baton with which Sullivan was provided so that his beat could be seen in the darkness of the ghost scene. The "portraits" in Act II were careful likenesses of the members of the company.

There are the standard role stereotypes again, though there was a new departure in Mad Margaret in which Jessie Bond was costumed as a half-naked gypsy. Here, there are obvious similarities to Ophelia, who also possessed a great deal of sense despite her apparent delusions.

On the whole the music lacks a lyrical element, apart from Dame Hannah's reunion with Sir Roderic, and Rose's Viennese lilt in "If somebody there chanced to be". Its place is taken by narrative or patter songs. The strong sense of the style of folk-song and 18th century air, already present in *Patience*, lies behind "I know a youth" and the "blameless" little country dance for Despard and Margaret in "I once was a very abandoned person". There is a preponderance of Sullivan's repeated chord accompaniments, but the orchestral writing is fine throughout, especially the virtuoso flute part in Margaret's "Cheerily carols the lark". The whole score is overshadowed by the highly dramatic ghost music with its tremolos, chromatic descents and *Freischütz*-like atmosphere. There is

also more than a hint of Weber in the chorus of bridesmaids.

The opera's problems began with its challenging title. This was originally spelt *Ruddygore*, which mealy-mouthed Victorian society could not stomach. Gilbert, when defending his choice, pointed out with his usual irrefutable logic – "'I admire your ruddy countenance', could mean 'I like your bloody cheek'!" Nevertheless, "y" soon became "i".

Although not regarded as a success, the opera ran far longer than *Princess Ida* – Gilbert said he would not mind more failures like this, but was tired of comparison with its immediate forerunner. He felt he should have called it *Kensington Gore*, or *Not So Good as the Mikado*. The first night was a disaster, at the end of which booing was heard in the Savoy for the first time. Two of the machines raising the pictures in the transformation scene broke down, and the second revivification of the ghosts proved to be an anti-climax. The end of the opera was promptly rewritten the next day, making Sir Roderic the only ghost to be finally brought alive.

The press took its cue from the audience: "The joint we have enjoyed hot from the spit may still be relished when presented cold with pickles. But when we find it persistently served up again … our palled palate revolts at it". Again the music was praised more than the libretto. The *Musical World* said "many parts of the ghost scene might well be transplanted into serious opera".

The collaborators were never to have total confidence in each other again, despite the successes to come. The differences in aspiration were becoming more marked. Sir Arthur Sullivan, England's finest composer of serious classical music and one of her best conductors, felt he was slumming when writing the Savoy operas. It was a pity that he needed money for his enjoyable life in high society, let alone his gambling. Meanwhile, Gilbert, with no illusions about his genius, was equally certain that he was providing the professional theatrical fare the public demanded.

SYNOPSIS

A chorus of out-of-work professional bridesmaids is hopefully singing of Rose Maybud's charms – she is, as yet, unmarried, despite the adoration of every young man in her Cornish village. Dame Hannah, her old aunt, says that she herself will never marry, having left her fiancé when she discovered he was Sir Roderic Murgatroyd, one of the accursed baronets of Ruddigore. She sings of the legend of the evil Sir Rupert, the founder of the line who was cursed by a witch: his descendants are forced to commit a crime a day until, glutted with sin, they beg to die. Rose enters, laden with totally inappropriate gifts for the village poor, and determined to judge all she meets by the rules of her personal Bible, a book of etiquette. The strictures of this code are clearly the reason why she is fancy-free, as she explains in her song "If somebody there chanced to be".

Nevertheless, when the bashful young farmer, Robin Oakapple, sings with Rose of "a youth who loves a little maid" they obliquely declare their feelings for each other. Robin, as it now transpires in his conversation with Old Adam, his servant, is really Sir Ruthven Murgatroyd, but has so successfully disguised himself that the hated title of Ruddigore has passed to his younger brother, the evil Sir Despard, who believes him dead.

The bridesmaids gushingly welcome Dick Dauntless, an archetypal Jack Tar and Robin's foster-brother, to the village. Dick boasts of his latest naval encounter with a French frigate, which he patronisingly dismisses as a "darned Mounseer". The foster-brothers greet each other joyfully; on hearing of Robin's shyness in asking Rose's hand, Dick offers to woo her by proxy. Robin bemoans the fate of the pathologically shy ("My boy you can take it from me"). Dick, however, is so taken by Rose that he wins her for himself, as she bends the rules of etiquette to suit the occasion, and they rejoice together ("The battle's roar is over"), encouraged by the bridesmaids, who scent employment at last. Their determined interjections of "Hail the Bridegroom, Hail the Bride" pepper Dick's explanation to Robin that Rose is now his. She vacillates between the two in the trio "Sailing o'er life's ocean wide", but eventually decides on Robin. As they depart, Mad Margaret enters with a crazed "Cheerily carols the lark" and a ballad "To a garden full of posies". She loves Sir Despard despite his reputation and is clearly jealous of Rose, whom Sir Despard has decided to carry off as his next victim.

The bridesmaids are attracted by the swaggering bucks and blades of Sir Despard's entourage ("Welcome gentry"), but Sir Despard himself reveals that the strain placed on its recipients by the curse of the Murgatroyds is clearly not to be envied. Nevertheless, today's crime is to be the abduction of Rose, just as Mad Margaret had feared. Dick, however, provides a way out for the reluctant bad

"How dreadful when an innocent heart becomes perforce a bad young Bart". Martyn Green, now revealed as Sir Ruthven Murgatroyd, and Radley Flynn, as his faithful servant Old Adam, bemoan their fates at the start of Act II (far left top).

"I once was as meek as a new-born lamb". Green's expression is decidedly more villainous in this publicity still (far left below).

"You understand? I think I do". Dick Dauntless betrays his foster-brother's identity to Sir Despard in Act I (above).

"Painted emblems of a race". The Murgatroyd ancestors descend from their picture frames and confront the terrified Robin (Act II) (left).

"RUDDIGORE"
An impression of Act I by H. M. Brock.   [Reproduced by permission of "The Sphere."]

"Silent is he for he's modest and afraid". Robin explains his natural diffidence to the understanding Rose (Act I) (top).

Old Adam entreats his master not to force him to "carry off a lady" (Act II) (Middle).

"Had your honour a brother?" Dick approaches Sir Despard (Act I) (above).

"In bygone days I had thy love". Rose pleads with Robin, while Dick and the chorus of bridesmaids look on (Act II) (right).

baronet with his disclosure of Robin's true identity ("You understand? I think I do"), thus securing Rose for himself, as it is certain she will not marry a villainous "bad bart." The wedding party enter, but the mood set by the chorus "Hail the bride of seventeen summers", Rose's "When the buds are blossoming" and the ensuing gavotte, is shattered by Sir Despard's unmasking of his long-lost brother and Robin's admission ("As pure and blameless peasant") that he is the reluctant heir of Ruddigore. Rose immediately offers to become Sir Despard's bride, but he, as a newly reformed character, rejects her for his first love, Mad Margaret. Rose promptly reverts to Dick and all seem happily paired off together, except for the wretched Robin ("For happy the lily").

At the beginning of Act II, Robin and Adam, now suitably villainous in appearance, are surrounded by the portraits of the past baronets of Ruddigore in the castle picture gallery ("I once was as meek as a new-born lamb"). Robin, however, is finding it difficult to commit really evil crimes; when Dick and Rose's wedding procession appears, he has not the heart to abduct her after she reminds him that "In bygone days I had thy love". He begs his ancestors for understanding, but, as the stage darkens, the ghostly baronets descend from their picture frames and warn Robin that he cannot escape his fate. Nevertheless, even ghosts can enjoy themselves; the spectral Sir Roderic gloats over the "ghosts' high-noon" which occurs "When the night wind howls in the chimney cowls". Robin is interrogated as to the nature of his crimes to date and subjected to a little light torture until he agrees to carry off a lady, and to pardon his forbears ("He yields! He answers to our call"). Duly absolved, the ghosts change back into pictures, and Robin steels himself to evil deeds (the number "Henceforth all the crimes that I find in *The Times* is cut in modern performance).

A soberly dressed Sir Despard and a practically sane Margaret appear, married, and now busy as joint heads of a "National School". Margaret's occasional vagaries can be checked by the utterance of the mystic word "Basingstoke". They call on Robin to reform and he, in the trio "My eyes are fully open to my awful situation", is determined that "it really doesn't matter" if he dies as long as his conscience is clear once more. Meanwhile Adam has abducted Dame Hannah, who, brandishing a dagger, is determined to defend her honour. Robin, terrified, calls on Sir Roderic, who becomes visible from the waist upwards. He and Hannah greet each other ecstatically by pet-names, and sing of their past love ("There grew a little flower"). Robin now finds the solution, however convoluted, to all problems. A baronet's refusal to commit a crime is tantamount to suicide, which is a crime in itself, so Sir Roderic should never have died at all and can be reunited with Hannah. Robin claims Rose, and Dick settles for Zorah, one of the bridesmaids, in the final ensemble ending with a reprise of "For Happy the Lily".

"My boy, you can take it from me". Robin explains to Dick that his natural modesty stops him from declaring his true feelings for Rose (Act I) (top).

"Let the welkin ring". The chorus of bridesmaids hails Dick's return from the wars (Act I) (Centre).

The Act I madrigal (above).

THE YEOMEN OF THE GUARD

OR THE MERRYMAN AND HIS MAID
SAVOY THEATRE (3 OCTOBER 1888) 423 PERFORMANCES

DRAMATIS PERSONAE

SIR RICHARD CHOLMONDELEY, *Lieutenant of the Tower* .... MR W BROWNLOW

COLONEL FAIRFAX, *under Sentence of Death* .... MR COURTICE POUNDS

SERGEANT MERYLL, *of the Yeomen of the Guard* .... MR RICHARD TEMPLE

LEONARD MERYLL, *His Son* .... MR W R SHIRLEY

JACK POINT, *A Strolling Jester* .... MR GEORGE GROSSMITH

WILFRED SHADBOLT, *Head Jailor and Assistant Tormentor* .... MR W H DENNY

THE HEADSMAN .... MR RICHARDS

FIRST YEOMAN .... MR WILBRAHAM

SECOND YEOMAN .... MR MEDCALF

THIRD YEOMAN .... MR MERTON

FOURTH YEOMAN .... MR RUDOLPH LEWIS

FIRST CITIZEN .... MR REDMOND

SECOND CITIZEN .... MR BOYD

ELSIE MAYNARD, *A Strolling Singer* .... MISS GERALDINE ULMAR

PHOEBE MERYLL, *Sergeant Meryll's Daughter* .... MISS JESSIE BOND

DAME CARRUTHERS, *Housekeeper to the Tower* .... MISS ROSINA BRANDRAM

KATE, *Her Niece* .... MISS ROSE HERVEY

CHORUS OF YEOMEN OF THE GUARD, GENTLEMEN, CITIZENS, &C.

SCENE – Tower Green

DATE – 16th Century

PLAYER'S CIGARETTES.

THE .HEADSMAN.
"THE YEOMEN OF THE GUARD."

The grim headsman of
the Tower of London is
eventually cheated of his
prey in the most serious of
the Gilbert and Sullivan
operas (above).

"O thoughtless crew".
Grahame Clifford, as
Jack Point, enters centre
stage to begin the opera's
Act II finale in the 1940
revival (top right).

Winifred Lawson, as
Elsie Maynard, faints into
the disguised Fairfax's
arms at the end of Act I
in the 1922 revival
(bottom).

AFTER the end of *Ruddigore*'s run, there was no new opera ready to replace it. Meanwhile, Alfred Cellier, whose brother, François, was D'Oyly Carte's musical director, had composed an enormous successful light opera *Dorothy,* with the young Marie Tempest in the title role. It ran for over 900 performances, longer than any Savoy opera had done, and Sullivan was worried, despite Gilbert's optimism. Carte's reaction was typical: he would raise his standards and build a larger theatre, making a "fresh start". Only revivals were being mounted, however, and Sullivan eschewed, rather than chewed, any preferred "Lozenge" plots.

The final inspiration lay on the draughty platform of Uxbridge station! Gilbert saw a poster there, advertising the Tower Furnishing Company resplendent with a Beefeater. It triggered the partnership's most three-dimensional and serious opera. "Pretty story, no topsy-turvydom, very human and funny also" pronounced Sullivan. The two men believed that it was their finest work to date, though later critics have felt that it spans too many genres and styles. Gilbert himself wanted to make it a "romantic and dramatic piece" to reflect the increasing seriousness of his plays. Above all, he showed himself unusually amenable to Sullivan's suggestions.

The plot has many similarities with Wallace's *Maritana* as *The Musical Times* pointed out, while the plot of Offenbach's *La Perichole,* which had shared the bill with *Trial by Jury,* also contained a blindfold marriage. Critics have noticed many plot implausibilities, while the pseudo-Tudor serious language is almost comic today. Additionally, *The Yeomen of the Guard* differs from all the other Savoy operas in that there is no actual satiric target and very little reference to contemporary events.

The characterisation contained within the piece has always held an audience, however. The tragi-comic figure of Jack Point, with its layers of folk and Shakespearean association is a compelling one, especially as it has an autobiographical element. The *Bab Ballad, Jester James* (1879), tells of a jester who has run out of jokes, and Gilbert himself often felt overwhelmed by his mantle of public buffoonery. Whatever Point is – and he has been played in various different ways – he is never merely sentimental. There are obvious similarities, too, with Shakespeare's fools, especially in his ability to coat unpalatable truths in nonsense. However, the poignancy of the tears behind the laughter is eternally moving.

The other characteristics are more fully fleshed than usual. Phoebe is honest and brave, while Elsie has remarkable probity in her faithfulness. Dame Carruthers is a kind of wise woman and Shadbolt is a parody of the usual melodrama villain, but all are believable human beings, however unbelievable the circumstances in which they find themselves.

Rehearsals were again shadowed by Gilbert's painful gout and so were often acrimonious, while Sullivan was becoming increasingly distressed by his partner's martinet behaviour in the theatre. In-

deed Gilbert's old-womanish fussing on the first night nearly unnerved Jessie Bond, who, as Phoebe, had to sing the opening song
of the opera. The nervous Gilbert kept asking how she felt, until she
pleaded to be left alone, as otherwise she would not be able to utter
a note.

On one occasion, however, Gilbert did come to Sullivan's aid.
The latter was finding the setting of the future show-stopper "I
have a song to sing-O" very difficult and asked Gilbert what had
suggested the words to him. Gilbert hummed a shanty often sung
by the crew on his yacht and Sullivan went straight to the piano and
improvised the song. "Only a rash man ever asked me to hum, but
the situation was desperate," said Gilbert.

The press approved of the music, although Sullivan felt they
were not as enthusiastic as he had hoped. The brass leitmotiv for
the Tower of London in the overture, which recurs in the Act I
finale and in Dame Carruthers' song near the beginning of the
opera, was remarked on in particular. This overture, unlike many, is
Sullivan's own composition, although not written until the final re-

"Here's a man of jollity".
Jack Point is featured on
the original publicity
poster for the first
performance. He is one of
Gilbert's most complex
characters and the story of
how he is "outwitted" still
makes its mark in modern
performance.

hearsal. Much of the scoring is characteristic of its composer as in the pizzicato cellos and muted violins accompaniment in "Were I thy bride". The usual contrapuntal deftness is present in such songs as Point's "A Private Buffoon", while there is the standard ensemble of perplexity in "When a wooer goes a-wooing".

The reviews also compared Sullivan with Schubert; the *Daily Telegraph*, for one, felt he was "Composing melody so pliant that it fits to every fold of the text, and so subtle that it seems to spring out of the words instead of being applied to them". The *Globe* pointed out the beauty of the madrigal "Strange Adventure" and the *St James' Gazette* felt that the opera catered for all tastes, being "music for musicians but quite tuneful enough and popular enough to please a mixed audience". Again, Gilbert had a much tougher time, as only the inconsistencies in the plot were noticed by *The Times*, who felt that the success of the piece was largely due to Sullivan's score. Above all the *Daily Telegraph* felt that it was "a genuine English opera, forerunner to many others, let us hope, and possibly a sign of an advance towards a national lyric stage". This comment confirmed that Carte's vision was becoming reality.

SYNOPSIS

The curtain rises to reveal Phoebe, daughter of Sergeant Meryll of the Yeomen of the Guard, sitting weeping at her spinning wheel on Tower Green. She hints at her love for the condemned Colonel Fairfax to the infatuated and jealous head jailor, Wilfred Shadbolt. The Yeomen and rest of the chorus march in, describing their role as tower warders in the autumn of their life. The Tower housekeeper, Dame Carruthers, Meryll (who owes his life to the colonel) and Phoebe all praise Fairfax's bravery and mourn his imminent decapitation that very day; Dame Carruther's sings vividly of the grim tortures that the Tower has seen over the centuries ("When our gallant Norman foes"). Meryll's hopes that his son, Leonard, may bring a reprieve for Fairfax, are dashed with Leonard's arrival. Father, daughter and son plot to disguise Fairfax in a Yeoman's uniform and pass him off as Leonard whom nobody has yet seen, and all three sing of the dangers ahead ("Alas! I waver to and fro"). The lieutenant of the Tower commiserates with Fairfax as he enters, guarded; however he faces his death with equanimity, asking "Is life a boon?"

Fairfax reveals that he has been convicted on a trumped-up charge of sorcery (he is an amateur alchemist), concocted by his cousin. As a last request, he asks to be married to the first available woman, so that he can cheat his rascally relative of his inheritance. A mocking crowd thrust in the jester, Jack Point and Elsie, a strolling player ("Here's a man of jollity"). Point manages to turn the threatening situation into a joke, and wins round the crowd in his poignant duet with Elsie "I have a song to sing, O" The lieutenant persuades Elsie to marry Fairfax ("How say you maiden, will you wed A man about to lose his head?"), and Point tries to impress the Lieutenant ("I've jest and joke") with his fooling. Meanwhile, Elsie has been married blindfold ("Tis done! I am a bride").

Phoebe now not only manages to steal the keys of Fairfax's cell and give them to her father while fascinating the lovelorn Wilfred with the possibilities of a life together ("Were I thy bride"), but to replace them after Fairfax's release. The latter enters beardless and in Yeoman's uniform, and is hailed by this chorus as the heroic Leonard Meryll. Phoebe is only too delighted to embrace him as a long-lost brother, and Wilfred commends her "To they fraternal care".

A solemn chorus enters ("The prisoner comes to meet his doom"), but the disguised Fairfax rushes back, having been ordered to fetch the captive, and reveals that the prisoner has escaped. Point despairs as his beloved Elsie tells him of her marriage to Fairfax, and the act ends with an agitated ensemble.

At the start of Act II two days later the chorus and Dame Carruthers are describing their vain search for Fairfax. Point enters, driven back on rehearsing old jokes from a large book, and finds an audience in Wilfred, who has pretensions to wit himself ("Oh! a private buffoon is a light-hearted loon"). He promises to teach Wilfred the secrets of the jester's trade if the latter will agree to swear that he shot Fairfax as he was trying to escape ("Hereupon we're both agreed"). Fairfax enters, feeling trapped at being tied to an unknown bride ("Free from his fetters grim"). Dame Carruthers, while caring for the shocked Elsie has learned of her secret marriage and she, her niece Kate, Fairfax and Meryll all muse on this "Strange adventure!", from which Fairfax deduces that his bride is the "winsome" Elsie. She enters and he declares his love for her, but she refuses him, thinking he is Leonard, and that she must be true to her vanished Fairfax.

A shot is heard and Wilfred and Point describe the mythical dispatch of Fairfax as he was swimming to freedom across the Thames. Point seizes his chance to try to woo Elsie, but is corrected on his approach by Fairfax in "A man who would woo a fair maid". The latter's demonstration of his technique is successful in winning Elsie, to the despair of Phoebe and Point. Wilfred catches Phoebe on the rebound and, having let slip the secret of Fairfax's disguise, she reluctantly agrees to marry him, if he keeps the secret as well.

Meanwhile the true Leonard appears with the delayed reprieve, but Dame Carruthers' silence must be bought with Meryll's reluctant hand ("Rapture, Rapture"). Elsie is horrified by the news, for she realizes that her impending marriage to "Leonard" would be bigamous, but her grief is turned to joy as she recognizes Fairfax as her lover. Point, in a reprise of "I have a song to sing, O," falls senseless to the ground with grief, as everyone rejoices around him.

"I have a song to sing O!" John Reed, one of the great players of Jack Point, first sang the role in 1952 (above).

All the great Jack Points have brought individual characteristics to the role. Currently, he is being played with a Welsh accent (top).

THE GONDOLIERS

OR THE KING OF BARATARIA

SAVOY THEATRE (7 DECEMBER 1889) 554 PERFORMANCES

DRAMATIS PERSONAE

THE DUKE OF PLAZA-TORO, *A Grandee of Spain* .... MR FRANK WYATT

LUIZ, *His Attendant* .... MR BROWNLOW

DON ALHAMBRA DEL BOLERO, *the Grand Inquisitor* .... MR DENNY

MARCO PALMIERI, *Venetian Gondolier* .... MR COURTICE POUNDS

GIUSEPPE PALMIERI, *Venetian Gondolier* .... MR RUTLAND BARRINGTON

ANTONIO, *Venetian Gondolier* .... MR METCALF

FRANCESCO, *Venetian Gondolier* .... MR ROSE

GIORGIO, *Venetian Gondolier* .... MR DE PLEDGE

ANNIBALE, *Venetian Gondolier* .... MR WILBRAHAM

OTTAVIO, *Venetian Gondolier* .... MR C GILBERT

THE DUCHESS OF PLAZA-TORO .... MISS ROSINA BRANDRAM

CASILDA, *Her Daughter* .... MISS DECIMA MOORE

GIANETTA *Contadine* .... MISS GERALDINE ULMAR

TESSA *Contadine* .... MISS JESSIE BOND

FIAMETTA, *Contadine* .... MISS LAWRENCE

VITTORIA, *Contadine* .... MISS COLE

GIULIA, *Contadine* .... MISS PHYLLIS

INEZ, *The King's Foster-Mother* .... MISS BERNARD

CHORUS OF GONDOLIERS AND CONTADINE, MEN-AT-ARMS, HERALDS AND PAGES

ACT I – The Piazzetta, Venice

ACT II – Pavilion in the Palace of Barataria

(An interval of three months is supposed to elapse between Acts I and II)

DATE – 1750

DESPITE ITS FINE MUSIC, *The Yeomen of the Guard* was not an unqualified public success, probably due to its audience's uncertain reaction to its tragi-comic mood. In addition, Sullivan was becoming preoccupied with Queen Victoria's suggestion – "You ought to write a grand opera, Sir Arthur – you would do it so well". In January 1889, he wrote to Gilbert firmly: "I have lost the liking for writing comic operas", while paying him the compliment of asking to to be his librettist for *Ivanhoe*, the projected English grand opera. Gilbert wisely refused, asserting that the librettist is always "swamped" in serious opera. The answer was aggressive – "You say that in a serious opera you must more or less sacrifice yourself. I say that this is just what I have been doing". Gilbert's explosive retort ended mildly. "You are an adept in your profession and I am an adept in mine. If we meet, it must be as master and master." Sullican maintained in a letter to Carte, which the latter tactlessly showed to Gilbert, "excepting during the vocal rehearsal, and the two orchestral rehearsals, I am a cipher in the theatre". The result was stalemate until May that year, when Carte persuaded the two men to meet. They "shook hands and buried the hatchet" and started work on *The Gondoliers*.

Gilbert took the word Barataria from *Don Quixote*, in which Sancho Panza was promised the governorship of this mythical island. The plot reverts to topsyturvydom in that it hinges, like *HMS Pinafore*, on baby-swopping, and the switching of rank. The other influence on Gilbert came from his reading on the subject of 15th-century Venetian republicanism.

Gilbert allowed himself a personal joke at the expense of the cast. Established Savoy "stars" like Jessie Bond had recently been demanding higher salaries, so he put the plot's egalitarian theme into practice by creating seven leading roles. Otherwise, the characters were the usual types; the Duke and Duchess can trace their origins back to Ko-Ko and Katisha, while the Inquisitor bears a more than passing resemblance to Pooh-Bah. Decima Moore, who created the role of Casilda at the age of only 18, recalled the kindness that both Gilbert and Sullivan showed in her audition. Gilbert even wrote this limerick about her:

"There was a young lady named Decima
Whose conduct was quoted as "pessima".
But her sins she forsook
And the sacrament took
On a Sunday they called Quinquagesima"

The music's sunny mood reflects a recent visit Sullivan made to Venice in its use of Italian folk dances: tarantellas and saltarellos jostle with other vivacious national dances, such as the cachuca, a fast gipsy dance from Granada, in Spain. There is even a snippet of a Scottish reel to accompany Don Alhambra's reference to "toddy" as well in "There Lived a King", while music for the blind man's bluff of Act I also has a traditional origin.

"From the sunny Spanish shore". The Duke and Duchess of Plaza-Toro, their daughter, Cassilda, and retainer, Luiz, arrive in Venice by gondola, as featured in this poster (above).

"In enterprise of martial kind". Martyn Green first played the part of the Duke in 1934 (top)

"Once more gondoliere".
A typically Gilbertian
topsy-turvy twist, in
which Luiz is revealed as
the rightful king of
Barataria, brings the
opera to a happy ending
as the gondoliers and
contadine set sail back to
Venice.

The second influence lay with other opera composers: the slithering chains of thirds (Rossini), *bel canto* in "Take a Pair of Sparkling Eyes" (Bellini), and the peasant elements in both Bizet's *Carmen*, and even Mozart (in *Don Giovanni* and the *Marriage of Figaro*). It was pointed out to Sullivan that "When a merry maiden marries" bore a resemblance to "Just a Song at Twilight" by James Molloy. Sullivan retorted that "you must remember that Molloy and I had only seven notes on which to work between us!" Above all, he luxuriated in composing an initial 18 minutes of music uninterrupted by dialogue. The whole opera glitters with the heady exuberance of Sullivan kicking up his musical heels – splendid cross-rhythms in

Marco and Guiseppe explain their "republican principles" – their father led "the last insurrection" – to an attentive Grand Inquisitor (Act I) (right)

"Thank you gallant gondolieri", mock-Handel in Don Alhambra's "There lived a King", and music with even more dazzling contrapuntal ingenuity for "In Contemplative fashion" that for the famous *Mikado* trio.

One of Gilbert's targets was very much in tune with the times. In the 1870s, Queen Victoria's unpopularity had led to the establishment of over 50 republican clubs in Britain, while the 1880s had seen the beginnings of socialism. Here, the subject of social equality is more fully aired than it was in *HMS Pinafore* or *Iolanthe* for the simple reason that it is taken to its logical conclusion. The Gondolier-kings do the work, but the court "equals" are still dissatisfied. The moral reached in all three operas is that people who insist on rank and etiquette still run the world.

Another target is limited companies with an "influential directorate". On its creation a limited company invites investors to buy its shares through a published prospectus, followed by an official allotment of shares. The Limited Liability Act, which was passed in the middle of the 19th century, laid down that, if a loss is incurred by such a company, the shareholders are liable only for the amount they invested. The Duke of Plaza Toro, in registering himself as such a company, was trying to raise capital by false pretences.

One other contemporary reference may be puzzling – the King of Barataria's conversion to Wesleyan Methodism. The original Methodist Holy Club had been founded by the Wesley family in the previous century, but the term "Wesleyan" was not used until 1858, and was a common subject of religious discussion.

There was journalistic rejoicing on the first night at the return of the prodigal duo to top form. "Gilbert has returned to the Gilbert of the past and everyone is delighted," said the *Illustrated London News*. "It is not opera or play, it is simply entertainment – the most exquisite, the daintiest entertainment we have ever seen," was another gushing comment. The *Sunday Times* described "Take a pair of sparkling eyes" as "one of Sir Arthur Sullivan's inspirations – a train of purest melody, exquisitely accompanied by divided strings pizzicati, in imitation of a guitar". A slightly more earthy note was struck by the *Topical Times:* "The attractions of the Gondoliers are numerous. To begin with the chorus wore comparatively short skirts for the first time, and the gratifying fact is revealed to a curious world that the Savoy chorus are a very well-legged lot."

On 6 March 1891, there was the final accolade of a Royal Command performance at Windsor Castle. Queen Victoria was seen to be beating time to "Then one of us will be a Queen" (which had been whistled from the gallery on the first night). She noted in her diary that the music was "charming", Jessie Bond was "a very clever little actress," but Barrington was "very fat".

The Gondoliers is the last of the "great" Savoy operas; the future was only illuminated by flashes of old alchemy in Utopia Ltd and The Grand Duke. Though written by Sullivan in haste as always, with the added handicap of the by now almost chronic pain of his kidney complaint, with a mind full of *Ivanhoe* as well as the recent major disagreement with his partner, the wit of the music enhances the libretto with as much effervescence as ever.

SYNOPSIS

"I stole the prince and I brought him here". Kenneth Sandford, as the Grand Inquisitor, explains how he abducted the infant son of the king of Barataria and brought him to the home of "a highly respectable gondolier" in Venice.

Act I opens in the piazetta in front of the Doge's palace in Venice. A chorus of 24 pretty girls (the contadine) are making posies, and waiting for Marco and Giuseppe, their favourite gondoliers, to come and choose their brides ("List and learn, ye dainty roses"). The gondolier chorus enters, led by Antonio; they are selflessly content to wait for the remaining 22 girls. Marco and Giuseppe jump ashore, and they and the girls greet each other ("Buon' giorno, signorine"). A duet follows ("We're called gondolieri") in which the two describe their almost honorary trade of "weary lagooning". They announce their intention of choosing two brides, but tactfully ask to be blindfolded, so that fate can decide their choice. After a game of blind man's buff, in which there is a certain amount of cheating, Marco catches Gianetta and Giuseppe catches Tessa. They nobly, if half-heartedly, offer to swop the girls, who indignantly protest at such rudeness, before singing a self-congratulatory thank-you and dancing off, hot-foot, to the altar.

The distinctly shabby Duke and Duchess of Plaza-Toro, with their daughter Casilda, and their drum-carrying attendant, Luiz, arrive ("From the sunny Spanish shore"), swearing that "They will never, never, never Cross the sea again". The first piece of dialogue follows, in which they establish their poverty by asking the unfortunate Luiz to conjure up halbadiers, a band ("sordid persons who require to be paid in advance") and to tootle like a cornet. Luiz's proffered farmyard imitations in lieu are scorned and he departs. The duke and duchess tell Casilda that she was married, as a baby, to the infant future King of Barataria, who was abducted soon afterwards and brought to Venice. He has now unknowingly succeeded to the throne, for his father has died in an insurrection. Meanwhile the duke hopes to retrieve his fallen fortunes by forming himself into a limited company. He launches into the customary biographical song (to the rhythm of a habanera) in which he relishes his cheerful cowardice as a military leader who always led his regiment from behind ("In enterprise of martial kind").

Immediately the duke and duchess have departed, Luiz and Casilda rush into each other's arms, but she tells him of her newly discovered marital status. He is puzzled, as the erstwhile nurse of the prince is his own mother, but they regretfully agree to part. The duke and duchess now usher in Don Alhambra Bolero, the Grand Inquisitor of Spain, who explains, after a little preliminary ogling of Casilda, that the new ruler of Barataria is here in Venice, living as a common gondolier with his supposed brother. His song ("I stole the

Prince") states that there is "no possible doubt whatever" that she is married to one of the two gondoliers, but as their father is dead, only their old nurse knows whose veins carry the true Baratarian blood, and at present she cannot be found.

The quintet decide to abandon themselves to fate on the lugubrious cue from Don Alhambra that "Death is the only true unraveller". At their departure, the chorus enter, singing of the joys of the newly-celebrated double marriage, and Tessa exults in her nuptial bliss ("When a merry maiden marries"). Don Alhambra overhears that Marco and Guiseppe are married and also that they are republicans. He explains that one of them is a king, but suggests royalty is compatible with their republican ideals. In Gilbert's world, however, ideals can quickly change with altered circumstances, so the gondoliers decide to sail immediately to claim their kingdom jointly and "abolish taxes and make everything cheap, except gondolas". Don Alhambra forbids the girls to accompany them, until the identity of the king is discovered, and after an initial protest from Gianetta ("Kind sir you cannot have the heart") they agree to part temporarily and look forward to the future ("Then one of us will be a Queen") and true equality ("For every one who feels inclined"). The gondoliers depart by boat, leaving the contadine.

Act II sees Marco and Giuseppe ensconced, regally attired, in Barataria, busily cleaning the royal regalia and surrounded by their court of gondoliers, who are all amusing themselves without any social distinctions. Giuseppe sings of the gratifying pleasures of being a true working monarch ("Rising early in the morning"), but they lack the recipe for perfect happiness, which is Marco's "Take a pair of sparkling eyes". On cue, Tessa and Gianetta run in, with the

A *golden moment from the 1929 revival. Henry Lytton is seen as the Duke of Plaza-Toro, Bertha Lewis as the Duchess and Sylvia Cecil as Cassilda. The sets and costumes are by Charles Ricketts (above).*

"*I am a courtier grave and serious*". The Plaza-Toro family demonstrate to Marco and Guiseppe the correct way of observing court etiquette in Act II (top)

"*Small titles and orders*". By Act II, the Duke of Plaza-Toro has been rescued from his poverty by being floated as a limited company. He is now "*blazing in the lustre of unaccustomed pocket money*" (above).

contadine. They are enthusiastically welcomed, and inundate their husbands with excited wifely questions, each taking alternate lines, but are told that until the aged nurse of the infant king appears, nobody knows who is truly king. They all dance a cachucha, which is interrupted by Don Alhambra. Horrified at the brazen lack of social distinctions, he moralises "When everyone is somebodee, Then no one's anybody" ("There lived a King"). He announces the arrival of the Plaza-Toros, and reveals that Casilda is the wife of whichever gondolier is king. The bewildered quartet try to make sense of the situation ("In contemplative fashion").

The Plaza-Toros, enter, magnificently attired as befits a limited company and its dependents. Casilda fears she will only feel duty, not love, for her unknown husband, but her mother reminds her ("On the day when I was wedded") that love can be forced if one is determined enough, even for such an unlikely subject as the duke. He and the duchess revel in their rather shady acquisition of wealth ("Small titles and orders"). They chide the gondoliers on their lack of court etiquette which they try to teach them ("I am a courtier grave and serious"). On their exit, the new married couples and Casilda endeavour to try and solve the riddle of two husbands and three wives. All is resolved as Don Alhambra enters with Inez, the infant prince's nurse, who declares that, when traitors came to abduct the prince, she substituted her own son for Luiz, who is in fact the rightful monarch. He and Casilda rush into each other's arms, the gondoliers and contadine prepare to return to Venice and general joy is expressed in a reprise of the cachucha.

UTOPIA LIMITED

OR THE FLOWERS OF PROGRESS

SAVOY THEATRE (7 OCTOBER 1893) 245 PERFORMANCES

DRAMATIS PERSONAE

KING PARAMOUNT THE FIRST, *King of Utopia* .... MR RUTLAND BARRINGTON

SCAPHIO, *Judge of the Utopian Supreme Court* .... MR W H DENNY

PHANTIS, *Judge of the Utopian Supreme Court* .... MR JOHN LE HAY

TARARA, *The Public Exploder* .... MR WALTER PASSMORE

CALYNX, *The Utopian Vice-Chamberlain* .... MR BOWDEN HASWELL

IMPORTED FLOWERS OF PROGRESS

LORD DRAMALEIGH, *A British Lord Chamberlain* .... MR SCOTT RUSSELL

CAPTAIN FITZBATTLEAXE, *First Life Guards* .... MR CHARLES KENNINGHAM

CAPTAIN SIR EDWARD CORCORAN, K.C.B., *of the Royal Navy* .... MR LAWRENCE GRIDLEY

MR GOLDBURY, *A Company Promoter – afterwards*

        Comptroller of the Utopian Household .... MR SCOTT FISHE

SIR BAILEY BARRE, Q.C., M.P., ... MR ENES BLACKMORE

MR BLUSHINGTON, *of the County Council* .... MR HERBERT RALLAND

THE PRINCESS ZARA, *Eldest Daughter of King Paramount* .... MISS NANCY MACINTOSH

THE PRINCESS NEKAYA *Her Younger Sister* .... MISS EMMIE OWEN

THE PRINCESS KALYBA, *Her Younger Sister* .... MISS FLORENCE PERRY

THE LADY SOPHY, *Their English Gouvernante* .... MISS ROSINA BRANDRAM

SALATA, *Utopian Maiden* .... MISS EDITH JOHNSTON

MELENE, *Utopian Maiden* .... MISS MAY BELL

PHYLLA, *Utopian Maiden* .... MISS HOWELL-HERSEE

ACT I – A Utopian Palm Grove

ACT II – Throne Room in King Paramount's Palace

A FTER the ennervating effects of the "carpet quarrel" of 1890 (see Chapter 4), both Gilbert and Sullivan had tried working with other collaborators, but neither felt as inspired by their new partners as they had been by each other. Meanwhile, Queen Victoria had ordered command performances of *The Mikado* and *The Gondoliers*, which reaffirmed the artistic strength the two men could muster together. So they tried again.

There is certainly plenty of satire in *Utopia Limited*'s mockery of English customs, some of it as biting as Gilbert had ever written. He mocks meaningless social ceremonial, as in the "Court of St James' Hall" debutante reception, where the highest in the land sing and play like Christie (black and white) Minstrels. His introduction of the extra touch of tea and "a plate of cheap biscuits" here was amusingly taken up by the real court. The original idea for the plot probably came from William Morris' *News From Nowhere* of 1891 which was subtitled *A Utopian Romance*. In making the earthly paradise of Utopia – and its inhabitants – into limited liability companies, Gilbert was attacking the Joint Stock Company Act of 1862, though his target here was already somewhat dated. Zara's political forecast, however, predicting that "One party will assuredly undo all that the other Party has just done" is as relevant today as it was in 1893. There is, incidentally, an amusing reference to the contemporary popular song Tarara-Boom-De-ay, in the name of Tarara, the Public Exploder.

There is so little lyricism in the libretto that Sullivan found setting it very hard and slow work. The music is, as a result, less sentimental and in many ways wittier and drier, leavened by the *Liebslieder* waltz rhythms that characterize the Utopians. It is a measure of Gilbert's new mildly cooperative spirit that, when Sullivan was having difficulty setting Act II, he offered to add words to the music, in burlesque fashion. Their public reassertion of creative harmony led to a touching end to the first night when a sick Sullivan and a gout-crippled Gilbert tottered on to the stage and shook hands to the audience's vociferous delight.

The opera received a mixed press. The always contrary Shaw liked the music the best of all the Savoy operas, comparing it, in places, to Mozart's *Cosi fan Tute*. Other press reports veered from the ecstatic to *Punch*'s assertion that the piece did not rise above the commonplace. The *Musical Times* felt it was "reminiscent rather than fresh", whereas the *Musical Standard* thought the orchestration "delicate, subtle and ingenious". All enjoyed the minstrel music. As for the libretto the *Pall Mall Gazette* felt it was a "mirthless travesty" of Gilbert's usual work "It is always a melancholy business when a writer is driven to repeat himself ... The quips, jests, the theory of topsy-turvy, the principle of paradox, the law of the unlikely seem to have grown old in a single night". Gilbert had not lost his wit, but perhaps he was now writing to a formula, and was no longer guided by his instinctive sense of what was effective theatre.

S Y N O P S I S

Act I opens with the chorus singing of their lotus existence "In lazy langour – motionless" in the palm court of King Paramount of Utopia's palace. They are apprehensive at the announcement of the return of Princess Zara, from her English education at Girton, for she is determined to anglicize their tropical paradise. Various characters then introduce themselves. First comes Tarara, the Public Exploder, whose job is to temper Paramount's despotism by blowing him up if he oversteps the mark. He produces the local gossip sheet *The Palace Peeper,* which is full of the king's misdeeds and complains to Scaphio and Phantis, the two Wise Men of the realm, that he is being thwarted in fulfilling his public duty (in fact, we soon learn that the reports are actually written by Paramount himself at the Wise Men's behest). Paramount, in fact, is the most virtuous of despots (In every mental lore). Phantis confesses that he is in love with Zara, even though he is an unsuitable 55, while Scaphio rallies him ("Let all your doubts take wing").

Paramount and his court appear. As a benevolent despot ("A King of autocratic power we"), he orders his twin daughters, Nekaya and Kalyba to be on show. They declare "Although of native maids the cream, We're brought up on the English scheme". They demonstrate the virtues of their education, directed by their English governess, Lady Sophy, in "Bold faced ranger". Left alone with the two Wise Men, the King muses on the humour of a rule that is only despotic in appearance ("First you're born"). However he is disturbed by Lady Sophy's discovery of *The Palace Peeper.* She cannot understand why he has not punished the perpetrator, and he promises to consult the Mikado as to the punishment most suitable for such a crime! She is convinced he loves her in their duet "Subjected to your heavenly gaze," but refuses him.

Zara is escorted to meet her father by Captain Fitzbattleaxe and the overheated First Life Guards in "helmet hot" (a strong reminiscence of *Princess Ida*). In the eventful ensuing ensemble, Fitzbattleaxe and Zara reveal their love, the Life Guards are very taken with Utopian feminity, while Scaphio, too, falls in love with Zara, much to the horror of Phantis. The two explain their rivalry to the captain and Zara; the former offers to hold her in trust for them until they have fought a duel to settle which is to have her hand ("It's understood all round").

Zara now confronts the unfortunate Paramount with *The Palace Peeper.* He explains to her that he is a despot in name only and that ultimate power lies firmly in the collective hands of Scaphio and Phantis. Zara's answer is immediate. She introduces her Flowers of Progress, imported from England, as the solution to the problem. They are Sir Bailey Barre, a prominent barrister, Lord Dramaleigh, the puritanical Lord Chancellor, Mr Blushington, a County Councillor, Mr Goldbury, a company promoter, and Captain (now Sir

Edward) Corcoran, an obvious refugee from *HMS Pinafore*. Mr Goldbury explains how he will turn Utopia itself into a limited company – "Some seven men form an Association" – and all are dazzled by his sales talk into instant agreement.

Act II begins with an (irrelevant) showstopper. Fitzbattleaxe sings of the trials of "A tenor all singers above" who cannot reach the statutory top C. He and Zara congratulate themselves on the progress that the Flowers have brought to the island, before breaking off for a duet "Words of love too loudly spoken". The king and the Flowers assemble for Zara's royal reception of Utopian debutantes in the manner of a Drawing Room held in the "Court of St James' Hall" (a popular music hall of the time). They range themselves to perform like Christy Minstrels, while the king rejoices that "Society has quite forsaken all her wicked courses".

After the young ladies have been presented, the two Wise Men announce "With fury deep we burn" at the ruin of all their schemes by the Flowers. The king is different to their threats to blow him up in the trio "If you think that when banded in unity". He points out that "you may Wind Up a Limited Company. You cannot conveniently Blow it Up". All three dance to express their varying moods. Frustrated, Scaphio and Phantis enlist Tarara to defeat the Flowers ("With wily brain upon the spot").

Dramaleigh and Goldbury are delight with the Drawing Room reception especially the innovative tea and biscuits provided. Goldbury describes the feminine ideal of "an English girl of eleven stone two" to the exaggeratedly demure Nekaya and Kalyba, who are most relieved to find that "Art is wrong and Nature right". Lady Sophy, in contrast, bewails her "over-conscientious heart" in describing her search for a "spotless king" to love. But she and Paramount decide they do love each other, after he has confessed to his authorship of *The Palace Peeper* ("Oh the rapture unrestrained"). After a joyous dance, in which the others join, the rebels, led by Tarara and the two Wise Men, burst upon the scene, at the end of which Zara has to admit that there is something missing from the Utopian scheme. She decides that government by party is the missing link, and Utopia will no longer be "a Monarchy (Limited) but a Limited Monarchy". The Wise Men are led off and all join in a celebration of England's virtues.

THE GRAND DUKE

OR THE STATUTORY DUEL
SAVOY THEATRE (7 MARCH 1896) 123 PERFORMANCES

DRAMATIS PERSONAE

RUDOLPH, *Grand Duke of Pfennig Halbpfennig* .... MR WALTER PASSMORE

ERNEST DUMMKOPF, *A Theatrical Manager* .... MR C KENNINGHAM

LUDWIG, *His Leading Comedian* .... MR RUTLAND BARRINGTON

DR TANNHÄUSER, *A Notary* .... MR SCOTT RUSSELL

THE PRINCE OF MONTE CARLO .... MR SCOTT FISHE

VISCOUNT MENTONE .... MR CARLTON

HERALD .... MR JONES HEWSON

THE PRINCESS OF MONTE CARLO, *betrothed to Rudolph* .... MISS EMMIE OWEN

THE BARONESS VON KRAKENFELDT, *betrothed to Rudolph* .... MISS ROSINA BRANDRAM

JULIA JELLICOE, *An English Comédienne* .... MDME ILKA VON PALMAY

LISA, *A Soubrette* .... MISS FLORENCE PERRY

OLGA, *Member of Ernest Dummkopf's Company* .... MISS MILDRED BAKER

GRETCHEN, *Member of Ernest Dummkopf's Company* .... MISS RUTH VINCENT

BERTHA, *Member of Ernest Dummkopf's Company* .... MISS JESSIE ROSE

ELSA, *Member of Ernest Dummkopf's Company* .... MISS ETHEL WILSON

MARTHA, *Member of Ernest Dummkopf's Company* .... MISS BEATRICE PERRY

CHAMBERLAIN, NOBLES, ACTORS, ACTRESSES, &C.

ACT I – Public Square of Speisesaal

ACT II – Hall in the Grand Ducal Palace

DATE – 1750

AFTER *Utopia Limited*'s respectable failure, Gilbert had found another younger composer, Frank Carr, for his new libretto, *His Excellency.* "If it had had the benefit of your expensive friend Sullivan's music, it would have been a second Mikado," he wrote to Helen D'Oyly Carte, and indeed the libretto was good, but the music weak. Sullivan, meanwhile revised the 20-year-old *La Contrabandista* under a new title, *The Chieftain,* but using the same librettist, Burnand, with whom he had written *Cox and Box.* His other theatrical effort, the incidental music to *King Arthur,* was, according to Shaw "penn'orths of orchestral sugar-stick". So, at Carte's instigation, the two ageing giants wheeled wearily round to face each other again. Neither man had lost his talent – they had merely lost their joint alchemy. Unfortunately in their last and worst opera, they were to prove this conclusively.

Gilbert was always in touch with current theatrical trends, of which the Ruritanian theme was certainly a popular one in the 1890s, perhaps as a result of the success of Anthony Hope's novel, *The Prisoner of Zenda.* As long ago as 1853, Gilbert had read a story called *The Duke's Dilemma* in *Blackwoods Magazine,* which had a suitably topsy-turvy theme of an impoverished Duke pretending to be rich (shades of the Plaza-Toros) to impress his fiancée, who engages a troup of actors to impersonate his court. In 1889 this story was adapted as a play with the title *The Prima Donna.* It has also been suggested that a newspaper article about a resuscitated, erstwhile dead person's legal rights, prompted the idea of the statutory duel, fought by drawing cards, where the loser is technically "dead".

There was a great deal of argument over the casting, and, in the end, a young German singer, Ilke von Palmay, was given the inflated plum role of Julia Jellicoe. This unusual device was dictated by a Gilbertian infatuation. In general, the opera's satire was spiteful, rather than effective, hitting at Queen Victoria's Hanoverian accent, and at the pretensions of minor royalty in general. The story is extremely confused and, for the first time, the rhyming is laboured – "ghoest", for example, is forced to rhyme with "lowest". Gilbert was all too aware of the new opera's failings, calling it "the ugly misshapen little brat", while Sullivan said, with unwonted directness, "Another week's rehearsal with WSG and I should have gone raving mad".

The *Standard* critic said the obvious. "It is absurd of course to expect a mine to be workable for ever . . . the mine is giving out." He went on to point out that, "Mr Gilbert is more Gilbertian than ever, and Sir Arthur Sullivan more Sullivanesque" but that "the net result is parody and distortion" and that "the rich vein which the collaborators . . . have worked for so many years is at last dangerously near exhaustion".

Gilbert and Sullivan never spoke again, though they took a joint curtain call at the revival of *The Sorcerer* under Sullivan's baton on

2 November 1898. Sullivan wrote in his diary "we went on together but did not speak to each other". Any creative communication had ceased too since *The Gondoliers* – for the sad last few years they co-existed, rather than collaborated.

SYNOPSIS

A group of actors, in the Ruritanian Grand Duchy of Pfennig Halb-pfennig, are enjoying a premature wedding breakfast in honour of the "pretty wedding" scheduled for the following day between Lisa and Ludwig, their juvenile leads. The happy couple sing of their love ("Pretty Lisa fair and tasty"), but the company have other things on their minds. They are conspiring to dethrone the excessively mean Grand Duke, who himself is to be married the next morning to the enormously wealthy Baroness von Krakenfeldt. As a sign of mutual recognition, all the conspirators have to eat a ritual sausage roll. Their manager, Ernest Dummkopf, who expects to succeed to the throne after the duke's deposition, claims that his life as a theatrical manager is ideal preparation for his new role ("Were I king in very truth"). To his delight, and despite her dislike of him, his English leading lady, Julia Jellicoe, insists that if Ernest is going to be Grand Duke, she must play the Grand Duchess.

An agitated Ludwig rushes in, describing how "Ten minutes since, I met a chap" who ate three sausage rolls, and was therefore given full details of the deposition plot. This hearty eater turned out to be not a fellow conspirator, but the Duke's private detective, so the plot has been revealed. The Notary suggests the answer is a statutory duel ("About a century since"), in which the loser – the drawer of the lowest playing card – is deemed dead for 24 hours, and so can be safely denounced as leader of the plot. As the law governing the duel runs out on the morrow, the loser can promptly come to life again and escape punishment. All praise the solution ("Strange the views some people hold"), the cards are drawn and Ludwig wins with an ace, thus deposing Ernest as manager.

The thin, frail and poorly dressed Grand Duke Rudolph enters, averring, in his introductory song, that he is "A pattern to professors of monarchical autonomy" because he is excessively miserly. He announces the details of the wedding, and explains to the baroness that his existing betrothal to the infant Princess of Monte Carlo, will only become void if she marries before she comes of age (at 2 pm the next day), so they must be married before this hour. They look forward to the pleasures of married bliss, when they will enjoy scrimping and saving together ("As o'er our penny roll we sing"). On opening his detective's report, Rudolph confesses that, as "a broken-down critter", he is not strong enough to cope with another conspiracy; he wishes he could be dead till it is over. The obvious answer, as Ludwig now suggests, is a rigged Statutory Duel, which is then elaborately staged with many exaggerated insults between

A gallery of characters from some of the key Gilbert and Sullivan operas. The creative partnership between Gilbert, Sullivan and Carte created a school of true comic opera, which will never die (above).

Rudolph and Ludwig, who "wins" as arranged, and immdiately extends the duel law by a century, so that he can remain on the throne. What he has not foreseen is that Julia, as leading lady, will stand on her contract and demand that she, not Lisa, shall now be the Duchess.

Act II begins with the return of the company, dressed in their Troilus and Cressida costumes, from Ludwig and Julia's marriage ceremony. Ludwig announces "At the outset I may mention" that all will become "early Attic" in style. Lisa begs Julia to "Take care of him". Alone, Julia and Ludwig plan how, as actors they will play their married roles ("Now Julia Come"). They are interrupted by the company and a furious baroness, who says that, as Grand Duke Ludwig has taken on all Rudolph's responsibilities, including herself as his bride.

Meanwhile, Ernest is bored with being "technically dead", but when he meets Lisa and then Julia they are terrified, thinking he is a ghost. Having reassured Julia, he tries to persuade her to marry him. Their duet "If the light of love's lingering ember" is interrupted by Ludwig and the Baroness' wedding procession, followed hotfoot by a herald announcing the arrival of the Monte Carlo court, whose "magnificent array" is misleading, for they, too, are impecunious. Ludwig is puzzled, as he has never heard of the betrothal, and already has three ladies with claims to his hand.

The situation is resolved by the notary's announcement that the winning aces in the Statutory Duels count as the lowest, not the highest, cards in the pack and the status quo is therefore restored. Ludwig and Lisa, Ernest and Julia and Rudolph and the Princess all happily pair off and dance away to their weddings.

Chronological Tables

MANY OF THESE FACTS FROM JAMES TRAGER THE PEOPLE'S CHRONOLOGY HEINEMANN 1979

DATE	GILBERT AND SULLIVAN	THE ARTS	THE WORLD
1836	Gilbert born 18 November	Donizetti's L'Elisir D'Amore Meyerbeer's Les Huguenots Mendelssohn's St Paul Dickens' Sketches by Boz	Battle of the Alamo
1837		Carlyle's French Revolution Dickens' Pickwick Papers Dickens' Oliver Twist Berlioz's Requiem	Queen Victoria comes to throne Beginnings of economic depression Morse invents his telegraphic system Euston station opens

1838		Donizetti's Lucia di Lammermoor
		Popular tunes Annie Laurie and Flow
		   Gently Sweet Afton
			1st transatlantic steamship crossings
			Regent's Park opens
			Irish Depression begins
			Anti-Corn Law league founded by
			   Cobden

1839			General growth of railways First Aintree meeting Rugby rules devised
1840		Donizetti's La Fille du Régiment Browning begins to write	Victoria and Albert married Darwin's Voyage of the Beagle 1st Cunard ship voyages 1st postage stamps (Penny Black) Afternoon tea made fashionable by Duchess of Bedford Hypnosis discovered Mass emigration of Irish to US
1841		Launch of New York Tribune and Punch Illustrated London News founded Verdi's Nabucco Wagner's Rienzi Mendelssohn's 3rd symphony	London population at 2.24 million Ether used for anaesthesia
1842	Sullivan born 13 May		Chartist movement starts
1843		Balfe's Bohemian Girl Theatre Regulation Act passed Macmillan opens his first bookshop Wagner's Flying Dutchman Turner's Sun of Venice Mendelssohn's Midsummer Night's Dream First negro Minstrel group show	SS Gt Britain launched Typewriter invented Appearance of 1st Xmas cards Nelson's column built

1844	Carte born 3 May	Dumas' Three Musketeers
		Disraeli's Coningsby
		Verdi's Ernani
			Laing's National Distress written on the
			   effects of industrialisation
			Marx announces religion is "the opium
			   of the people"
			YMCA founded
			1st Morse telegraph message sent out

1845		Disraeli writes The Two Nations Schumann's piano concerto Mendelssohn's violin concerto Wagner's Tannhauser	Engels' Condition of the working class in England Franklin dies looking for NW passage
1846		Covent Garden re-building Edward Lear's Book of Nonsense Landseer's Stag at Bay	Potato famine continues Corn laws repealed Invention of standard railway gauge

DATE	GILBERT AND SULLIVAN	THE ARTS	THE WORLD
1846		Mendelssohn's Elijah	Invention of pneumatic tyre Invention of ice-cream
1847		C. Brönte's Jane Eyre Sweeney Todd Verdi's Macbeth British Museum opens	Ether first used in British surgery Bank of England nearly fails Further potato famine in Ireland and economic depression widespread
1848		Pre-Raphaelite Brotherhood founded Thackeray's Vanity Fair Dumas' La Dame aux Camélias	Revolutions in Paris, Vienna, Prague, Rome Chartist movement revives First attempt to legislate sanitation Waterloo station opens

1849		Edgar Allen Poe dies
		Millais' and Holman Hunt's first Pre-
		   Raphaelite paintings
		Johann Strauss the elder dies
			Californian Gold Rush
			Roman republic declared under Mazzini
			   and supported by Garibaldi
			Cholera epidemic in London
			Bowler hat invented
			Harrods founded
			Reinforced concrete patented

1850		Dickens' David Copperfield
		Wagner's Lohengrin
			Invention of the Bunsen burner
			Singer sewing machine invented
			Free trade principles embraced in
			   Britain and food tariffs removed
			New prosperity and rising wages
			Last salmon caught in Thames – too
			   polluted afterwards
			Tea overtakes coffee in popularity

1851		1st publication of Fun
		New York Times founded
		H.B. Stowe's Uncle Tom's Cabin
		Melville's Moby Dick
		Boucicault's Dame de Pique
		Verdi's Rigoletto
		Christy Minstrels publicize Old Folks
		   at Home
			Great Exhibition
			End of French 2nd Republic
			Wet collodion process for developing
			   photographs invented
			Reuter news agency started
			London at 2.37 million declared world's
			   largest city

1852	Helen Lenoir born 12 May (not 1859 as previously thought)		Kerosene distilled
1853		Verdi's Rigoletto in London Ruskin's The Stones of Venice Dickens' Bleak House Mrs Gaskell's Cranford C. Bronte's Villette	Patenting of the safety match
1854	S. joins Chapel Royal	Le Figaro first published Tennyson's Charge of the Light Brigade	Crimean War broke out First distillation of petrol Vatican ruling of papal infallibility
1855		Verdi's Trovatore in London Kingsley's Westward Ho! Louvre opened	Livingstone discovers Victoria Falls Burton and Speke's explorations book YWCA founded Modernisation of London's sewers First domestic gas oven sold
1856	G. graduates and starts work as a clerk S. wins 1st Mendelssohn scholarship	Verdi's La Traviata Larousse Dictionary published First US copyright protection laws Bechstein and Wurlitzer produce first instruments	Crimean War ends Anglo-Chinese war begins

1857	G.'s commission to translate
	   Laughing Song
		Flaubert's Mme Bovary
		Dickens' Little Dorrit
		Arnold's Tom Brown's Schooldays
			Matrimonial Causes Act where husband's
			   responsibility fully described
			Poaching laws eased

DATE	GILBERT AND SULLIVAN	THE ARTS	THE WORLD
1857			Sepoy rebellion which ends East India Company's control of India
1858	S. goes to Leipzig	Offenbach's Orpheus in the Underworld where first can-can is danced Adelaide Ann Proctor writes poem The Lost Chord Mendelssohn and Wagner Marches at marriage of Princess Royal Covent Garden rebuilt	Assassination attempt on Napoleon III and Empress Eugenie Anglo-Chinese war ends Lecture on survival of the fittest by Darwin and Wallace Gray's Anatomy published Bernadette of Lourdes has her vision First transatlantic cable and President Buchanan and Queen Victoria exchange greetings Big Ben opened by the Queen First refrigerator invented
1859		Dickens' Tale of Two Cities Fitzgerald's Rubaiyat of Omar Khayam Manet's The Absinthe Drinker Steinway piano is manufactured	First petrol production in US Darwin's Origin of Species published War between France and Austria declared First Jewish member of House of Commons, Lionel Rothschild Building of Suez canal starts Cocaine isolated from cocoa leaves
1860	G. embarks on legal career	Eliot's Mill on the Floss Boucicault's The Colleen Bawn W. Collins' The Woman in White	Garibaldi uprising in Italy with his "redshirt" army Burke's expedition to Australia First pasteurisation of milk
1861	G. writes first Bab Ballads for Fun	Verdi's Un Ballo in Maschera in London Macaulay's History of England Dickens' Great Expectations Eliot's Silas Marner Reade's Cloister and the Hearth Palgrave's Golden Treasury First complete performance of Bach Mass in B minor Mrs Beeton's Book of Household Management	Prince Albert's death Unification of Italy American Civil War begins Russian serfs emancipated Pasteur's germ theory of disease Britain biggest coal and iron producer in the world
1862	S. is launched with The Tempest	Christina Rossetti's Goblin Market 2nd Great Exhibition in London (extensive Japanese displays)	Joint Stock Company Act (attacked in Utopia Limited) Abolition of slavery Speke finds source of Nile Britain runs out of cotton due to American Civil War Cotton and crop famine in Britain Crosse and Blackwell introduce canned soups
1863	S. meets Rachel	Gounod's Faust Manet's Dejeuner sur l'herbe Delacroix dies Bizet's The Pearl Fishers	London Underground opens
1864	S. becomes Staff Organist at Covent Garden	Offenbach's La Belle Hélène Verne's Journey to the Centre of the Earth Trollope's Small House at Allington	Charing Cross station opens Pullman invents railway sleeping car W.G. Grace begins his cricket career First fish and chip shops opened
1865	G.'s Christmas Extravaganza	L. Carroll's Alice in Wonderland Swinburne's Atalanta in Calydon Robertson's Society Wagner's Tristan und Isolde First performance of Schubert's Unfinished symphony	End of the American Civil War Lincoln assassinated Palmerston dies Mendel's laws of heredity expounded Origin of Salvation Army

DATE	GILBERT AND SULLIVAN	THE ARTS	THE WORLD
1866	S.'s father dies G.'s Dulcamara S. writes Cox and Box S. made RAM professor S.'s In Memoriam overture	Thomas' Mignon Tolstoy's War and Peace Swinburne's Poems and Ballads Manet's The Fifer Smetana's The Bartered Bride First Broadway musical The Black Crook William Morris's reclining chair	Invention of dynamite Cook's Tours begin
1867	Schubert MSS discovered by S. and Grove S.'s La Contrabandista Gilbert and Lucy Turner married	Trollope's Last Chronicle of Barset Cézanne's Rape Gounod's Romeo and Juliette Popular song Little Brown Jug by R.E. Eastburn Robertson's Caste Offenbach's La Grande Duchesse Verdi's La Forza del Destino Verdi's Don Carlos Blue Danube 1st performance	Marx's Das Kapital 2nd Reform Bill extending suffrage First dry cell battery invented Marquess of Queensbury boxing rules
1868	G.'s The Merry Zingara G.'s burlesque on Robert Le Diable	Hollingshead opens at the Gaiety Wagner's Meistersinger Brahms' German Requiem Strauss' Tales of the Vienna Woods	Disraeli comes to power then defeated by Gladstone in December Typewriter patent issued
1869	G. and S. meet S. composes The Prodigal Son G. writes Ages Ago	L. M. Alcott's Little Women Schubert C minor symphony performed Grieg's piano concerto Wagner's Das Rheingold	Girton College founded Suez canal completed Cutty Sark launched Abolition of British debtor's prisons Stanley sets off to find Livingstone Firm of Heinz is founded
1870	G.'s The Princess G.'s Palace of Truth Carte sets up his concert agency G.'s Our Island Home	Morris' The Earthly Paradise Verne's 20.000 Leagues under the sea D.G. Rossetti's House of Life Delibes' Coppelia Wagner's Die Walküre Tchaikowsky's Romeo and Juliet Wagner's Flying Dutchman	First bicycle Foundation of Red Cross Siege of Paris by the Germans Education Act
1871	G. and S.'s Thespis G.'s Pygmalion and Galatea Carte's first marriage S.'s Onward Christian Soldiers	Verdi's Aida Albert Hall opens Chopsticks composed by Arthur de Lulli	Newnham College founded Napoleon III deposed Purchase of British Army commissions abolished Franco-Prussian war ends The Paris Commune
1872		Lecocq's La Fille de Mme Angot Hardy's Under the Greenwood tree Samuel Butler's Erewhon L. Carroll's Through the Looking Glass Whistler's painting of his mother Degas Le Foyer de Danse Bizet's L'Arlesienne music Sarah Bernhardt begins her career and Eleanora Duse begins her career	George Smith's discovery of the Assyrian account of the Flood First motion picture invented First chewing gum invented Licensing Act to curb excessive drinking
1873	G.'s The Wicked World S.'s Light of the World	Walter Pater's Studies in the History of the Renaissance Verne's Around the World in 80 Days	Maxwell's treatise on electricity and magnetism Father Damien goes to his leper colony
1874	G.'s Charity G.'s Sweethearts	Hardy's Far from the Madding Crowd First French Impressionist exhibition Verdi's Requiem Moussorgsky's Boris Goudonov	Sir Garnet Wolesley ends the Ashanti war End of 1st Gladstone ministry Foundation London School for Medicine for Women Remington typewriter introduced Lawn tennis patented Agricultural depression in Britain

DATE	GILBERT AND SULLIVAN	THE ARTS	THE WORLD
1875	Trial by Jury G.'s Broken Hearts S.'s The Zoo	Wagner's Lohengrin performed in London in Italian Carl Rosa opera company founded Corot dies Bizet's Carmen Tchaikowsky's 1st piano concerto	Telephone invented by Alexander Graham Bell Suez canal comes under British control Liverpool Street station opened Matthew Webb 1st person to swim English Channel Liberty opens shop
1876	G.'s Dan'l Druce Syndicate founded Rupert D/C born S. becomes principal of future RCM S. awarded an Honorary Mus. Doc. from Cambridge	National Training School for music founded Verdi's Aida Renoir's Le Moulin de la Galette Grieg/Ibsen's Peer Gynt Frist complete performance of Wagner's Ring Brahms' 1st symphony	Queen Victoria made Empress of India Invention of commercial paint Invention of "Lily the Pink's" compound for "women's ills" Dewey originates his system Player piano invented
1877	The Sorcerer G.'s play Engaged First agreement with Carte Helen Lenoir joins company S. begins relationship with Fanny Ronalds S.'s brother Fred dies S. writes The Lost Chord	Tolstoy's Anna Karenina Tchaikowsky's Swan Lake Saint-Saens' Samson and Delilah	Women allowed to practise medicine Russia declares war on Turkey First telephone sold Last restrictions on freedom of Press lifted at Bradlaugh/Besant trial along with ban on giving contraceptive advice First Wimbledon tennis matches
1878	H.M.S. Pinafore	Bizet's Carmen in London Word "jingo" introduced in a music hall song Hardy's The Return of the Native Henry James The Europeans	Victor Emmanuel II dies Edison Electric Light Co. formed Tiffany glass factory begun Jehovah's witnesses founded Cleopatra's Needle erected on the Embankment World's 1st birth-control clinic opens in Amsterdam
1879	The Pirates of Penzance S. has kidney stone operation S. awarded honorary Oxford degree G. and S. visit America The Pinafore fight on 31 July	Kate Greenaway's Under the Window H. James' Daisy Miller Tchaikowsky's Eugene Onegin Brahms' violin concerto Dvorak's Slavonic Dances	Edison's light bulb publicly shown Pavlov's experiments on animal behaviour Woolworth's founded British wheat crop failure and Irish potato famine again
1880	S.'s Martyr of Antioch S. becomes conductor of Leeds Festival	Dostoievsky's Brothers Karamazov	Koch vaccination against anthrax First newspaper photos First successful shipment of frozen Australian beef to England
1881	Patience G.'s Foggerty's Fairy Carte's first wife dies Savoy built Electric light used in the Savoy	Offenbach's Tales of Hoffman H. James' Portrait of a Lady	Assassination of Alexander II Irish agitate for Home Rule under Parnell Venetian gondola outmoded by vaporetto Death of Disraeli
1882	Iolanthe S.'s mother dies	Wagner's Tristan and Meistersinger in London Oscar Wilde's arrival in New York Manet's Bar at the Folies Bergères D.G. Rossetti dies a drug addict Ibsen's Ghosts Wagner's Parsifal Smetana's Ma Vlast	Street lighting by electricity begins Daimler invents internal combustion engine Koch discovers the TB bacillus First psychoanalysis experiments Married Women's Property Act passed
1883	5 year agreement between G., S. and Carte S. Knighted	Nietzsche's Thus Spake Zarathustra Stevenson's Treasure Island Delibes' Lakmé	Invention of the machine gun First Buffalo Bill's Wild West Show

DATE	GILBERT AND SULLIVAN	THE ARTS	THE WORLD
1884	Princess Ida	Twain's Huckleberry Finn Seurat, Cézanne, Gaugin and Van Gogh support Les vingt Popular song Love's Old Sweet Song Massenet's Manon	First linotype typesetting machine Cocaine used as an anaesthetic Foundation of Fabian Society 1st fountain pen invented by Waterman 1st ABC teashop opened
1885	Mikado	Wagner's Parsifal in London Meredith's Diana of the Crossways Pater's Marius the Epicurean R. Haggard's King Solomon's Mines Stevenson's A Child's Garden of Verses Van Gogh's The Potato Eaters Ibsen's The Wild Duck Johann Strauss's The Gipsy Baron	Daimler invents petrol engine Fabian society founded Benz produces 1st gasoline car General Gordon dies in Khartoum Lord Salisbury temporarily defeats Gladstone Pasteur discovers anti-rabies vaccine

1886	S.'s The Golden Legend	Cellier's Dorothy
		Hardy's Mayor of Casterbridge
		H. James' The Bostonians
		Stevenson's Kidnapped and Dr Jekyll
		    and Mr Hyde
		Corelli The Romance of Two Worlds
		Millais' Bubbles
		8th Impressionist exhibition
		Rodin's The Kiss
		C. Franck's Symphonic variations
		Moussorgsky's Night on a Bare Mountain
			Gladstone returns briefly then is replaced
			    by Salisbury over Home Rule
			Gold rush to the Transvaal
			Coca-Cola is sold as headache remedy

1887	Ruddigore	Haggard's She and Allan Quartermain Kipling's Tales from the Hills Van Gogh's Moulin de la Galette Strindberg's The Father Verdi's Otello Chabrier's Le roi malgré lui Rimsky-Korsakov's Cappriccio Espagnol Moussorgsky's Pictures at an Exhibition	Lloyds of London founded

1888	The Yeomen of the Guard
	S.'s incidental music to Macbeth
	Carte marries Helen
	Command performance of S.'s The
	    Golden Legend
		Van Gogh's Sunflowers
		Rodin's Thinker
		Fauré's Requiem
			Kaiser Wilhelm II mounts German throne
			Dunlop obtains patent for a pneumatic
			    bicycle tyre
			Pasteur Institute founded
			Burton's 1001 Arabian Nights
			Kodak camera introduced
			Jack the Ripper murders
			Invention of Esperanto
			Edison invents the phonograph

1889	The Gondoliers	Verdi's Otello in London
		Van Gogh's Starry Night
		Van Gogh's Self Portrait
		C. Frank's Symphony in D minor
		Yamaha founds musical instrument
		    making company
		Strindberg's Miss Julie
			Rhodes becoming established in the
			    Transvaal
			Cleveland Street scandal about homo-
			    sexual brothel and P. of Wales
			Great London Dock strike establishes
			    trade unionism
			First milking machines
			Savoy Hotel opens
			Orient express's 1st journey

1890	"Carpet" quarrel	Frazer's Golden Bough
		Emily Dickinson's Poems
		Doyle's The Sign of Four
		Van Gogh dies
		Tschaikowsky's Sleeping Beauty
		Borodin's Prince Igor
		Tchaikowsky's Queen of Spades
			Bismarck resigns
			Rhodes becomes Prime Minister of the
			    Cape Colony
			Java Man remains found
			Hollerith's punch card processing
			First electric underground railway in
			    London

1891	S.'s Ivanhoe G.'s Rosencrantz and Guildernstern	Hardy's Tess of the D'Urbevilles Wilde's Portrait of Dorian Grey	

DATE	GILBERT AND SULLIVAN	THE ARTS	THE WORLD
1891	Command performance of Gondoliers Command performance of Mikado	Morris' News from Nowhere 1st Toulouse Lautrec posters Seurat dies Ibsen's Hedda Gabler Cinder-Ellen (contained Tarara- Boomdeay)	
1892	S.'s Haddon Hall G.'s The Mountebanks	Shaw's first play Widower's Houses Wilde's Lady Windemere's fan C. Doyle's 1st Sherlock Holmes book Kipling's Barrack-room ballads B. Thomas' Charley's Aunt Leoncavello's Pagliacci Tchaikowsky's Nutcracker Suite H. Dacre's song Daisy, Daisy	Gladstone takes over from Salisbury French invent 1st car with pneumatic tyres
1893	Utopia Limited	Pinero's The 2nd Mrs Tanqueray Munch's The Cry and The Voice Wilde's A Woman of no Importance Verdi's Falstaff Humperdinck's Hansel and Gretel Tchaikowsky's Pathétique symphony Dvorak's New World symphony S. Jones's A Gaiety Girl – 1st musical comedy Pop song Happy Birthday to you	Nansen explores Greenland Wall Street collapses Keir Hardie founds Labour party First Ford car Wrigley introduces chewing gum Lizzie Borden murder trial

1894		Shaw's Arms and the Man
		Verdi's Falstaff in London
		Du Maurier's Trilby
		Hope's Prisoner of Zenda
		Memoirs of Sherlock Holmes
		Kipling's Jungle Book
		Beardsley edits The Yellow Book
		Degas' Femme a sa toilette
		Yeats' Land of Heart's Desire
		Massenet's Thaïs and Werther
		Debussy's L'Après Midi d'un Faune
			Earl of Rosebery takes over from
			  Gladstone
			Nicholas II comes to Russian throne
			Manchester Ship canal opened
			Marks and Spencer starts
			Survey of Bethnal Green children
			  indicates starvation

1895		Wilde's Importance of being Earnest Wilde's An Ideal Husband Conrad's Almayer's Folly Hardy's Jude the Obscure Wells' Time Machine Corelli's Sorrows of Satan Tchaikowsky's Swan Lake Mahler's Resurrection symphony Strauss' Till Eulenspiegel	Discovery of the X-ray Freud's Studies in hysteria Randolph Hearst builds his empire Marconi pioneers wireless telegraphy First cinema shows Invention of the Gillette razor Cordon Bleu cooking school opens
1896	The Grand Duke	Houseman's A Shropshire Lad Millais dies Wilde's Salome Chekhov's The Seagull Puccini's La Bohème Dvorak's cello concerto	Rhodes resigns Shah of Persia assassinated Radioactivity discovered New Klondike gold rush Marconi's 1st permanent wireless installation on Isle of Wight Olympic Games re-started
1897		Bram Stoker's Dracula Rousseau's The Sleeping Gypsy Grand Guignol Theatre opens Dukas' The Sorcerer's Apprentice Sousa's Stars and Stripes	Moss Bros founds hire business

1898	S.'s The Beauty Stone
	Last public appearance of G. and S.
	  together
		H. James' Turn of the Screw
		Wilde's Ballad of Reading Gaol
		Stanislavski founds the Moscow Arts
		  Theatre and Method acting
			Dreyfus cleared in his re-trial
			Isolation of radium by Marie Curie
			Joshua Slocum sails round world

DATE	GILBERT AND SULLIVAN	THE ARTS	THE WORLD
1899	S.'s The Rose of Persia	Kipling's Stalky and Co. Gaugin's Two Tahitian Women Sisley dies Chekhov's Uncle Vanya Elgar's Enigma Variations O Sole Mio popular song S. Joplin's Maple-Leaf Rag	Boer War begins Aspirin and sticking plaster invented
1900	Sullivan dies 22 November	Colette's First Claudine novel Picasso's Le Moulin de la Galette Puccini's Tosca Elgar's Dream of Gerontius	Kitchener takes over Boer war command Chinese Boxer rebellion Umberto I of Italy assassinated Lenin returns to Russia from exile Freud's Interpretation of Dreams Paris Metro service begins First Zeppelin flies Birmingham University founded Brownie camera introduced Houdini's escapes begin HMV trademark appears

1901	Carte dies 3 April	Kipling's Kim
		T. Mann's Buddenbrooks
		Toulouse-Lautrec dies
		Rachmaninov's 2nd piano concerto
		Elgar's Pomp and Circumstance march
			Queen Victoria dies
			Theodore Roosevelt is youngest
			    American president after assassination
			    of President McKinley
			Roentgen wins first Nobel prize for
			    X-ray discovery

1902			Boer war ends
1906	First rep season begins	Galsworthy's Man of Property Sasson's Poems Vlaminck, Dufy, Derain creative Cézanne dies Caruso's first Victrola recording Maurice Chevalier becomes popular	HMS Dreadnought launched Jung meets Freud Word "allergy" coined Dreyfus restored to former rank Excavation of Panama canal Rolls-Royce firm founded San Francisco earthquake
1907	Gilbert knighted	Cubism with Braque and Leger Picasso's Demoiselles d'Avignon Synge's Playboy of the Western World Lehar's Merry Widow in London Pavlova dances Dying Swan	Dominion status granted to N Zealand Hoover vacuum cleaner invented
1908	2nd rep season begins	Forster's A Room with a View K. Grahame's Wind in the Willows Matisse and Chagall notorious Delius's Brigg Fair Elgar's 1st symphony Ravel's Rapsodie Espagnole	Geiger counter developed Asquith succeeds Campbell-Bannerman Model T Ford introduced Boy Scout movement begins
1911	Gilbert dies 29 May Fanny Ronalds dies	T. Mann's Death in Venice Beerbohm's Zuleika Dobson D.W. Griffith's films Strauss' Rosenkavalier Stravinsky's Petrouchka Pop song Alexander's Ragtime Band Beginning of true jazz Gropius' first buildings	Rutherford's nuclear model for atom Amundsen arrives at South Pole House of Lords loses veto powers
1913	Helen Carte dies	Proust's Swann's Way Lawrence's Sons and Lovers Shaw's Androcles and the Lion Schoenberg's Gurreleider Charlie Chaplin's 1st film contract Stravinsky's Rite of Spring	Emmeline Pankhurst imprisoned Schweitzer establishes Lambarene

Bibliography

ALLEN, Reginald   The First Night Gilbert and Sullivan N. York 1958

BAILY, Leslie   The Gilbert and Sullivan book (orig ed. Cassell 1952)

BAILY, Leslie   Gilbert and Sullivan and their world Thames and Hudson 1973

BEST, Geoffrey   Mid-Victorian Britain Weidenfeld and Nicolson 1971

BRADLEY, Ian   The annotated Gilbert and Sullivan 2 vols Penguin 1982

COX-IFE, William   W. S. Gilbert: Stage Director Dennis Dobson 1977

DARK, Sidney and GREY, Roland   W. S. Gilbert: his life and letters Methuen 1923

THE D'OYLY CARTE CENTENARY 1875–1975 Booklet produced by the Trust

DUNHILL, Thomas   Sullivan's Comic operas Edward Arnold and Co. 1928

EINSTEIN, Alfred   Music in the Romantic era Dent 1947

FREW, Gerald   "Oh yes it is!" BBC 1985

GAUNT, William   The Aesthetic Adventure Cape 1945

GILBERT, W. S.   Bab Ballads Macmillan 1964 ed.

GOLDBERG, Isaac   The Story of Gilbert and Sullivan N. York Simon and Schuster 1935 Crown Publishers

HARDWICK, Michael   The Osprey guide to Gilbert and Sullivan Osprey 1972

HAUGER, George   English musical theatre 1830–90 in Theatre Notebook no 2 1982

HUGGETT, Frank   Victorian England as seen by "Punch" Sidgwick and Jackson 1978

HUGHES, Gervase   The Music of Arthur Sullivan Macmillan 1960

HYMAN, Alan   Sullivan and his satellites Chappell 1978

HYMAN, Alan   The Gaiety years Cassell 1975

JACKSON, Stanley   The Savoy The Romance of a Great Hotel Frederick Muller 1964

JACOBS, Arthur   Arthur Sullivan OUP 1986

JACOBS, Arthur   Gilbert and Sullivan and the Victorians in Music Review 1951

JACOBS, Arthur   Gilbert and Sullivan Max Parrish 1951

JEFFERSON, Alan   The complete Gilbert and Sullivan opera guide Webb and Bower 1984

KOBBE'S   Complete Opera book rev ed 1987

LLOYD, Frederic   Nicolson 1984

LUMLEY, Benjamin   Reminiscences of the Opera 1884

MACKINLAY, Sterling   Origin and development of light opera Hutchinson 1927

MAITLAND, J. Fuller   English music in the 19th century 1902

MANDER, Raymond and MITCHENSON, Joe   A Picture History of Gilbert and Sullivan Vista Books 1962

NAYLOR, Gillian   The Arts and Crafts Movement Studio Vista 1971

NICHOLL, Allardyce   British Drama (originally 1925) Harrap

OXFORD COMPANION TO THE THEATRE   2nd ed OUP 1957

PEARSON, Hesketh   Gilbert: his life and style 1957

PEARSON, Hesketh   Gilbert and Sullivan Macdonald and Jane's 1975

RAYNOR, Henry   Sullivan reconsidered Monthly Musical Record xxxix 1959

ROE, F. Gordon   Victorian Corners Allen and Unwin 1968

ROLLINS, Cyril and WITTS, John   The D'Oyly Carte Opera Company in Gilbert and Sullivan Operas – A record of productions 1875–1961 Michael Joseph 1962

ROWELL, George   The Victorian Theatre 2nd ed 1978

ROWELL, George   Queen Victoria goes to the theatre Paul Elek 1978

SAVOYARD, The   Sept 1982 Iolanthe century issue Centenary number January 1975

SAVOYARD, The New   Vol 1 October 1988

SHAW, G.B.   Music in London 1890–4 1932

SHAW, G.B.   London Music 1888–9 as heard by Corno di Bassetto Constable 1937

SMITH, Geoffrey   The Savoy operas Robert Hale 1983

TRAGER, James   The People's Chronology Heinemann 1979

TRAUBNER, Richard   Operetta A Theatrical History Gollancz 1984

TREVELYAN, G.M.   Illustrated English History Vol 4 The Nineteeth Century Longmans originally 1949–52

WALKER, Ernest   A history of music in England 3rd ed. Clarendon Press 1952

WHITE, Eric Walter   The Rise of English opera

WILLIAMSON, Audrey   Gilbert and Sullivan opera Marion Boyars 1982

WILSON, Robin and LLOYD, Frederic   Gilbert and Sullivan The D'Oyly Carte years Weidenfeld and Nicolson

INDEX